THE INVISIBLE RELIGION

The Invisible Religion is a modern classic of social science. Its influence goes well beyond sociology as it continues to inspire research in such diverse fields as sociology of knowledge, ethnology, theology, sociology of religion, and religious studies. In this volume, the author endeavors to answer one of the most important questions regarding religion in modern times: Are Western societies indeed becoming more secular as they modernize? His surprising answer is still part of the ongoing debates about secularization as he argues that rather than a decline of religion, we are witnessing a shift from an older Church-centered form, to another invisible and still largely unexplored form of religion. Explaining why focusing only on Church when discussing religion is inadequate, this book presents a thorough case for reframing the question of the status of religion in modern life in a way that makes visible forms of religion hitherto unseen, and sketches some aspects of this new form. As such, it will appeal to sociologists with interests in social theory, religion, and the secularization thesis.

Thomas Luckmann was born in Jesenice, Slovenia and studied in Vienna and Innsbruck in Austria. From 1955 to 1965, he taught both at The New School and at Hobart College in New York. Returning to Europe, he became Professor of Sociology first at the University of Frankfurt, then at the University of Konstanz, where he remained until his retirement in 1994. The co-author of *The Social Construction of Reality* and *The Structures of the Life-World,* is regarded as one of the founders, with Peter L. Berger, of the 'new' sociology of knowledge.

Tom Kaden is a faculty member at the Institute of Sociology, University of Bayreuth, Germany. He is the author of *Creationism and Anti-Creationism in the United States of America* and the co-editor of *Science, Belief and Society: International Perspectives on Religion, Non-Religion and the Public Understanding of Science.*

Bernt Schnettler is Professor and Chair for Sociology of Culture and Religion at the University of Bayreuth, Germany. He is the author of the book on Thomas Luckmann in the German book series *Klassiker der Wissenssoziologie.*

Knowledge, Communication and Society

Series Editors

Bernt Schnettler
Universität Bayreuth, Germany
Hubert Knoblauch
Technische Universität Berlin, Germany
Michaela Pfadenhauer
University of Vienna, Austria
Alejandro Baer
University of Minnesota, USA

Knowledge, Communication, and Society: Contributions to the New Sociology of Knowledge seeks to revive the academic collaboration and debates between European and Anglo-Saxon currents of thought in the social sciences that characterised the middle of the last century, and provide a forum for the development of a new sociology of knowledge. A space for transatlantic discussion, it includes original works and translations of central works by contemporary European social scientists and is committed to an empirically grounded programme of developing social theory.

Titles in this series

Erving Goffman
From the Perspective of the New Sociology of Knowledge
Jürgen Raab

The Communicative Construction of Reality
Hubert Knoblauch

The New Art of Old Public Science Communication
The Science Slam
Miira B. Hill

The Invisible Religion
The Problem of Religion in Modern Society
Thomas Luckmann, edited by Tom Kaden and Bernt Schnettler

For more information about this series, please visit: www.routledge.com/sociology/series/KCS

THE INVISIBLE RELIGION

The Problem of Religion in Modern Society

Thomas Luckmann

Edited by Tom Kaden and Bernt Schnettler

Routledge
Taylor & Francis Group
LONDON AND NEW YORK

Published 2023
by Routledge
2 Park Square, Milton Park, Abingdon, Oxon OX14 4RN

and by Routledge
605 Third Avenue, New York, NY 10158

Routledge is an imprint of the Taylor & Francis Group, an informa business

Originally published in 1963 under the title *Das Problem der Religion in der modernen Gesellschaft* by Thomas Luckmann, Verlag Rombach, Freiburg im Breisgau (Deutschland). First English edition published in 1967 by The Macmillan Company, New York.

British Library Cataloguing-in-Publication Data
A catalogue record for this book is available from the British Library

Library of Congress Cataloging-in-Publication Data
Names: Luckmann, Thomas, author. | Kaden, Tom, editor. | Schnettler, Bernt, editor.
Title: The invisible religion : the problem of religion in modern society / Thomas Luckmann ; edited by Tom Kaden and Bernt Schnettler.
Other titles: Problem der Religion in der modernen Gesellschaft. English
Description: Abingdon, Oxon New York , NY : Routledge, 2022. | Series: Knowledge, communication and society | Includes bibliographical references and index.
Identifiers: LCCN 2022025921 | ISBN 9781032154039 (hardback) | ISBN 9781032191454 (paperback) | ISBN 9781003257875 (ebook)
Subjects: LCSH: Religion and sociology.
Classification: LCC BL60 .L813 2022 | DDC 306.6—dc23/eng20221026
LC record available at https://lccn.loc.gov/2022025921

ISBN: 978-1-032-15403-9 (hbk)
ISBN: 978-1-032-19145-4 (pbk)
ISBN: 978-1-003-25787-5 (ebk)

DOI: 10.4324/9781003257875

Typeset in Bembo
by Apex CoVantage, LLC

CONTENTS

EDITORS' INTRODUCTION

Bernt Schnettler and Tom Kaden

Not Invisible – But Unbound and Private: Luckmann's Sociological Theory of Religion Revisited

I

Religion is like suicide – at least in the very particular perspective inaugurated by one of sociology's founders.[1] When Émile Durkheim studied the role of suicide in late 19th-century France (Durkheim 2008), he emphasized the *sui generis* reality of collective behavior, and the unique sociological view of a phenomenon that, *prima facie*, would belong to a rather different research area, be it medicine, psychiatry, law, or moral statistics.

The same holds true for religion. One may ask if it should be studied scientifically at all. If one wants to preserve its aura, better not to investigate since disenchantment is the inevitable result of any thorough scrutiny. Luckmann, who remained a deeply devout Catholic throughout his life, would urge any sociologist never to argue with theologians. His warning points to a fundamental difference that separates sociology of religion from any other – scientific or lay – perspective on religion. First and foremost, it is *agnostic* regarding the content of religious belief. It is not the sociologists' task to defend, attack, justify, or delegitimate any of the belief systems members of any society may adhere to. In this respect, Luckmann's sociology of religion shares the Weberian credo of freedom from value judgment (Weber 2012). Sociology of religion establishes a unique view of what Luckmann conceives to be a universal human phenomenon. The variety of religions and belief systems that have evolved throughout history is manifestly evident. This fact demonstrates the richness of human cultures. History of religion and the anthropological study of religions contribute to the never-ending task of describing the fascinating abundance of human belief systems.

Sociologically, two main questions inform Luckmann's thinking on religion: What is the social origin, and what are the collective effects of religion, irrespective of specific religious beliefs, dogmas, and the variety of social organizations of religion. Consequently, sociology of religion in this sense depends both on anthropological and historical knowledge. It is not a specialized subfield dedicated to the study of the role of religion in society. Rather, in the line of thought represented here, sociology of religion is coextensive with the study of society as such, given the fundamental role of religion in socializing members into a collective moral order, of establishing ultimate meaning systems for any and all questions, and of legitimizing and stabilizing a particular way of life, an institutional order, and its associated world view.

II

After Thomas Luckmann's book *The Invisible Religion* was published in 1967, it engendered a significant development in the sociology of religion. Together with his close colleague and friend Peter L. Berger, coauthor of the book *The Social Construction of Reality* (Berger und Luckmann 1967), Luckmann generated a debate that initiated a decisive turn in the sociology of religion in the 1960s. It has come to be known as the start of the "neoclassic phase" that succeeded "church sociology." That impoverished version of a sociology of religion had been dominant during the decades following the early classical works of sociology at the turn of the nineteenth century. In the same year, Berger (Berger [1967] 1990) published the second crucial contribution to this paradigmatic shift in the sociology of religion based on the "new" sociology of knowledge developed by both authors. However, Berger's sociology of religion differs in important aspects from Luckmann's. Since the "neoclassical turn" which breaks with the ecclesiological narrowing in the postwar decades, and the nominalist approaches to definition associated with it, initiated by Berger's writing and Thomas Luckmann's *Invisible Religion*, the question of a sociologically appropriate definition religion has pervaded the disputes among sociologists of religion. The polarity between a "substantial" versus a "functional" understanding of religion serves as a guiding concept in this dispute. While the former is associated with the question of what the content of religion is, the latter is directed at what it provides for the individual or for society and its institutions. Not only sociologists have difficulties in conceptualizing the phenomenon of religion, as Falk Wagner's monumental study of the concept history reveals (Wagner 1991). Wagner speaks of "incomprehensibility in a double sense": Neither do we know exactly what religion is according to its concept, nor are we able to overlook the difficulties that impede a distanced and reasonable consideration of religion under the condition of its privatized character. To put it in a simplified way, religion is *functionally* defined by its effects and functions regarding the problems of the world of everyday life, by what it provides for the members of society, or for society as a whole. *Substantive* definitions, on the other hand, focus on the content of religion, asking what beliefs, religious experiences, transcendences, etc., characterize religion. In general, functional definitions emphasize the similarity between religion and other ideological systems, while substantive definitions emphasize the categorical difference between religious and "mundane belief systems." As a result, functional definitions are fundamentally in danger of losing sight of the specifically religious, and make it difficult to distinguish the religious from the non-religious. Substantive definitions, on the other hand, draw the boundaries much more narrowly. Due to the aforementioned conceptual-historical implications, they carry the dilemma of ethnocentric transfer to phenomena that are labeled as "religious" in other cultures and times, but do not correspond at all to the occidental understanding of religion.

III

The book reedited here is one of the modern classics in the sociology of religion. It has been translated into Italian (1969), Spanish (1973), Japanese (1976), Korean (1982), German (1991), Chinese (1995), Polish (1996), Slovenian (1997), Nowegian (2004), Portuguese (2014), and Turkish (2016). Surprisingly its English version has been out of print for decades although it is cited with continuous frequency. We are therefore pleased that, with this edition, the work will be available again to a wide readership.

Its author was a scholar rooted in academic circles on both sides of the Atlantic. Luckmann was quite familiar with the diversity of religion in Europe and in the United States. Part of his personal biography, not lacking in drama, was particularly beneficial for developing a sociological perspective on society and religion.

Thomas Luckmann (1927–2016) was born in Jesenice, Slovenia (in German: Assling), located between the Julian Alps and the Karawanks, in former Yugoslavia, close to the Austrian border. He was raised bilingually. His mother tongue was Slovene, his father spoke German. This helped him see the world from different angles. In this sense, he knew that reality is a *social construction* long before he and Berger wrote the book with that paradigmatic title (Berger & Luckmann 1967). Throughout his life, Luckmann maintained an extraordinarily broad intellectual scope, as is evidenced by his numerous fields of study and academic expertise. Luckmann studied philosophy and linguistics in Vienna and, later, Egyptology, psychology, French philology, and Church Slavonic in Innsbruck. His manifold interests led him to study at the New School for Social Research in New York, where he encountered important émigré scholars, such as Alfred Schutz and Karl Löwith. He graduated in 1953 and earned his doctorate in sociology in 1956. Subsequently, he was Teaching Assistant at Hobart College in Geneva, in upstate New York, later Chairman, before returning as a professor to the New School after the death of Schutz, where he remained until 1965, when he took a post at the University of Frankfurt. Repelled by the heated intellectual climate in Frankfurt during the turbulent years of the student revolution, Luckmann accepted a professorship at the newly founded University of Konstanz in 1970, located in the south of Germany at the border of the idyllic lake of Constance, where he taught until his retirement in 1994.

Luckmann's oeuvre covers a wide range of topics. They are anchored in interpretative social theory following Weber and Schutz. Luckmann's opus includes both works on general sociology, which decidedly follow classical conceptions, and contributions to methodology, as well as empirical research on temporality, identity, language, communication, and morality. In addition, Luckmann developed a theory of communicative genres.

Very early in his scholarly career, following his graduation, Luckmann took an interest in the social scientific study of religion. Among his first empirical works were sociological studies of religion conducted in postwar Germany.

IV

The Invisible Religion, originally published in 1967, is the substantially expanded retranslation of an earlier German book (Luckmann 1963a), in which Luckmann presented his theoretical framework for a sociological study of religion. There is a clear conceptual development in Luckmann's sociology of religion. One can observe that his early empirical studies of four German parishes (Luckmann 1959, 1956), and of evangelical academies in Germany (Luckmann 1957), were followed by his very critical review of works on the sociology of religion (Luckmann 1960). It was published in the leading German Journal of that time, the *Kölner Zeitschrift für Soziologie und Sozialpsychologie*, and caused an unusual amount of attention. In fact, it engendered a neoclassical turn in the sociology of religion (Wohlrab-Sahr 2000).

Das Problem der Religion in der modernen Gesellschaft, the 1963 German precursor of *The Invisible Religion*, is based, as he writes in the preface, on an unpublished English manuscript, remarkably titled *Notes on the Case of the Missing Religion*. In 1962, Luckmann delivered a keynote lecture at the annual meeting of the Society for the Scientific Study of Religion in New York, later published under the title "On Religion in Modern Society: Individual Consciousness, World View, Institution" in the *Journal for the Scientific Study of Religion* (Luckmann 1963b). In this article, his conceptual framework is already visible. Luckmann uses elements from phenomenology and philosophical anthropology for his theory of religion. This is combined with a basic functional understanding of religion, strongly oriented toward Durkheim.

Its starting point is fundamental criticism of the scope and theoretical orientation of the sociology of religion dominant at the time. Luckmann charges that postwar sociology of religion, in focusing on statistical analysis of service attendance and other church-related practices, basically identified religion with one particular social form of religion, namely, church religion, while being inattentive both to other possible forms of religion, as well as the underlying anthropological conditions that bring about a religious outlook in man. In *The Invisible Religion*, he sets out to correct both issues by laying bare those foundations, and by canvassing, in a broad historical sketch, subsequent dominant social forms of religion, and even hinting at the modern, privatized and individualized form that had started replacing church religion in his day.

V

Conceptually, Luckmann's understanding of religion is considered one of the most comprehensive ever: it is that "the basic function of 'religion' is to transform members of the natural species into actors in a historical social order" (supplement, p. 112). To Luckmann, religion is at the core of the individual's relation to society. For him, the forms of religion with which we are familiar are specific, institutionalized expressions of symbolic universes, i.e., socially objectified structures of meaning that relate to the everyday world, as well as realms of transcendence of everyday existence (p. 47). Religion ensures that society remains integrated because, as a symbolic reservoir of meaning, it supports the construction of social realities. Allotting religion this basic function means that religiosity is an indispensable feature of human existence, and religion a central feature of every social reality.

Since religion denotes a level of meaning that is removed from, and transcends, everyday life, it legitimizes the meaning of even the most mundane habits and actions of everyday life. This also means that the meaning religion represents is objectively binding, and cannot be questioned, which distinguishes it from other social forms of knowledge and instances of interpretation (such as science, economics, politics, law, or art). As a shared reservoir of meaning that secures and legitimizes interpretations and behaviors like no other, religion, therefore, "is immeasurably richer and more differentiated than the interpretive schemes that could be developed from scratch by individuals" (p. 54). Religion thus fulfills a rationalizing function for the individual by appearing as an expression of a universal order (p. 54).

Luckmann coined the term *Weltansicht* ("worldview") for this aspect of the function of religion. *Weltansicht* is the context of meaning that exists in any particular historical order or epoch. Of course, it can take different forms in different societies since there is a dialectical relationship between the *Weltansicht* and social structure. Worldviews in Luckmann's sense contain types and tropes, schemes of interpretation, and action; they form a unified "matrix of meaning" (p. 54) whose most important objective representation is language. To be clear, Luckmann does not say that all individual sense-making, each word of every language, etc., is religious in his sense. Rather, it is only a particular layer of meaning within this worldview, whose structural feature is that it orders everything else within it. It is, in a manner of speaking, the tip of the pyramid. Religion organizes the internal hierarchy of meaning of any worldview. Luckmann has repeatedly argued for such a functional view of religion because "[a] functional definition of religion avoids both the customary ideological bias and the 'ethnocentric' narrowness of the substantive definition of the phenomenon" (p. 46). Although he judges, somewhat apodictically, that substantive definitions are "of no value to sociology" (p. 46), it would be inappropriate to view Luckmann's sociology of religion as purely functionalist. To him, all particular religions are institutions with their own histories, while also tied back to the universal, anthropological foundation mentioned earlier. Part of his view of humans is that he identifies, as part of their biological constitution, the capacity for transcendence in a basic sense of transcending immediate experience. And it is this theory of transcendence, as part of his overall treatment of religion, that clearly bears "substantive" features. This becomes particularly clear in the supplement to the German edition of *The Invisible Religion* (*Die unsichtbare Religion*, Luckmann 1991), which is added in translation to this edition (see p. 110), and made available in English for the first time. In this addendum, Luckmann assigns greater importance to the experience of transcendence for his sociology of religion.

VI

Transcendence deals with the limits of the human life-world, and is closely linked with the fact that human existence is corporeal, and human experience has a particular structure. Among Luckmann's intellectual references in this context are German philosopher Edmund Husserl, who developed philosophical phenomenology around the turn of the 20th century (e.g., Husserl 2005); his teacher and colleague Alfred Schütz who further developed phenomenology as a social scientific paradigm (e.g., Schutz 1972b); German philosopher Helmuth Plessner (2019), who is most famous for his view of humans as possessing what he called "eccentric positionality"; and, finally, George Herbert Mead and his social psychological analyses of role-taking (Mead 2015).

Against this intellectual backdrop, Luckmann aims to make visible the structure of intersubjectivity as a transgression of boundaries. When born, the unfinished human being remains dependent on others, and becomes an individual only among his peers, for "the individuation of consciousness . . . is realized only in social processes" (p. 49). The precondition for this development is every person's ability to detach themselves from the ongoing events, stimuli, and reactions of their biological organism. This transcendence of biological nature, however, becomes possible only in the social context. In interaction with others, in which the individual finds herself "mirrored" in the behavior of others, she begins to see herself through the eyes of others, thus acquiring the ability to assume roles. Only then does she develop the ability to form an identity. The origin of religiosity lies in the experience of transcendence, in the task that naturally presents itself to each person to find access to that which they themselves are not. And it is due to this human disposition to religiosity that any particular religion exists as a socially institutionalized form of dealing with specific experiences of transcendence.

Taking up a typology already used by Schütz (Schutz 1972a), Luckmann identifies three levels, or kinds, of transcendence. Following Husserl's phenomenological analyses of consciousness, Schütz distinguished between "little," "intermediate," and "great" kinds of transcendence. According to Husserl, the transcendence of experience lies in the capacity of consciousness to "appresent." By this he means that our consciousness automatically adds meaningful complements to elements not contained in sense perception, e.g., to the perceived front sides of objects their back sides, etc. The instances of "little" transcendence occur in everyday reality when the present experience is transcended in time or space. For example, rising smoke as a "sign" points to a fire beyond the horizon, or a "sign" like the knot in a handkerchief points to a task to be done tomorrow.

The instances of "intermediate" transcendence refer to the social world of intersubjectivity. They differ from the experience of "little" transcendence in that what is experienced there is only ever indirectly accessible. While it is always possible, at least in principle, to close the gap between immediate experience and the object of "little" transcendence – one can walk toward the source of smoke until one encounters the fire – the boundary encountered in intermediate transcendence cannot even potentially be crossed. The thoughts of my fellow human beings are enclosed in an alien consciousness, which can at best be made communicable via certain "signs." The most important kind of signs are the words that make up natural languages, but encountering the inner state of another human through her words lets one perceive her inner state only indirectly.

Finally, instances of "great" transcendence are completely removed from everyday life. In extraordinary, non-everyday experiences, for example in dreams, visions and ecstasies, aesthetic experience, or in the visualization of death, the mundane reality of everyday life is transcended. Such extraordinary experiences form the reservoir from which religious worlds of meaning can be sustained. Since human perception and action are always tied to signs, they cannot be articulated with the expressive possibilities of ordinary language, and are conveyed by symbols and rituals. However, great transcendence does not establish religion by itself, because the interpretation of such experiences must first be inserted into a particular "theory of reality." Only when put in relation to everyday reality can these experiences be cast as belonging to another, "sacred," transcendental realm of reality. This is why visions can sometimes serve to justify new religions. Ultimately, it is culture that decides what effect the experiences of great transcendence can have, and whether they can be put into a meaningful context for those who have had such exhilarating, but sometimes also thoroughly frightening, experiences.

VII

In addition to the functional definition of religion as a social institution of meaning, and the theory of transcendence, *The Invisible Religion* contains a third aspect that is of great importance for cultural theory. It examines various specific social forms in which religion has been institutionalized throughout history. Luckmann's treatment of those social forms is necessarily brief and typological, leaving out many historical details and variants. He argues that in archaic societies, the division of labor and, thus, the differentiation between various social subsections is still very low. This entails a high degree of overlap between the individual and the social stock of knowledge. In this situation, religion, as a peripheral sacred realm, largely shapes the institutions that govern behavior. Religious patterns of interpretation provide unambiguous answers to the typical life crises that regularly intrude into the lives of individuals and groups. Only in traditional advanced cultures does the sacred cosmos exist with clear institutional separation from everyday life. The spread of written culture, and the production of economic surpluses, enable the emergence of experts who structure and codify the "higher forms of knowledge." In this way, religion gets a socially perceptible "basis" as an orderly, written system of interpretation, which establishes itself, first above, and later increasingly alongside, the other functional areas of society. Today's modern industrial societies are characterized by the sacred cosmos which once legitimized the entire society as an "official religious model," losing its influence on other institutional spheres. Influenced by thinkers such as Machiavelli, Galileo, Kant, and Smith, science, law, politics, economics, and other social spheres establish their own logic and rationality that no longer require a religious underpinning. Increasingly, institutionalized religion is losing its legitimacy and plausibility in people's lives. It is still taught, but its teaching often remains mere rhetoric, and its adoption as an "official model" degenerates into lip service at best.

VIII

Because of the aforementioned rapid differentiation of the social structure, the individual stock of knowledge and the social stock of knowledge increasingly diverge. This has consequences for the formation of personal identity, as well as for the "moral cohesion" of society. In dealing with these structural consequences of pluralization, another line of Luckmann's theory unfolds, which contains clear contemporary diagnostic, and even thoroughly "culture-critical," moments. Together with Peter L. Berger, he had already treated the problem of identity in *The Social Construction of Reality* (Berger und Luckmann 1967). In a lesser-known collaboration, the two scholars addressed the issue of religion and modernity as a form of "crisis of meaning" (Berger und Luckmann 1995). They agree that modernity has led to a radical change in the relationship between the individual and society and, therefore, also in religion. Pluralization is automatically accompanied by a weakening of the plausibility structures of the sacred cosmos, insofar as incompatible worldviews are available to – and cannot easily be ignored by – the individual. This not only concerns the pluralization of the "market of religions" – secular ideologies can sometimes also take over the function of religious systems of meaning.

However, given Luckmann's views on the anthropological foundation of religion and its function for the individual, it is not surprising that he vehemently opposes the idea that religion has completely left modern society. Not long after the publication of *The Invisible Religion*, he described secularization as a "contemporary myth" (Luckmann 1983). True, a certain social form of institutionalized religiosity (ecclesiasticism) does experience changes that can be characterized as secularization. But this by no means leads to a disappearance of religion altogether, because experiences of transcendence are universal components of human life, and religiosity is an anthropological disposition. Social change, therefore, cannot lead to the disappearance of religion, but merely to the emergence of new social forms that may not resemble traditional institutions and ideas. Also, secular ideologies such as communism, fascism, or anarchism may take over the function of religious systems of meaning. This may occur through adoption of aspects of institutionalized religions. On the other hand, a tendency toward the "privatization" of religion can be observed. Luckmann observes that religion is leaving church institutions, and expanding into the supposedly secular sphere of self-help groups, cliques, and other meaningful communities. Additionally, religiously relevant issues increasingly shift into the subjective realm. According to Luckmann, the "locus" of this new form of religion is the private sphere of the individuals themselves. In addition to the sacralization of the individual, the modern "sacred cosmos" contains themes such as self-realization, mobility ethos, family, and sexuality. The modern sacred cosmos is thus increasingly populated by themes that do not belong to the realm of "great" transcendence but to that of "intermediate" or even "little" transcendence. This leads individuals to conceive of themselves as the origin and source of religion. However, this tendency by no means leads to an isolated practice of religion by the individuals thus "sanctified." Rather, the traditional religions that continue to exist are joined by new social forms of religion that dwell in institutions such as psychoanalysis, therapeutic sects, and "New Age." These changes owe a lot to the emergence of new media and market-related forms of communication. Through television and the internet, the elements of the current individualized social form of religion are disseminated, perceived, and adapted to individual needs. The same communicative structure also has effects on the remaining traditional form of religion as evidenced by new forms of religious events, the rise of megachurches, widely popularized papal visits, and the like.

IX

Despite the 55 years that have passed since the original publication and this new edition, *The Invisible Religion* is a true sociological classic whose arguments directly or indirectly played a major role in many of the big disciplinary debates of the past decades.

Attempting only a rough overview, we identify three areas of scholarly engagement with Luckmann's thinking: the area of application and further development of Luckmann's perspective in *The Invisible Religion*; various forms of adaptation into other research perspectives, which sometimes include modifications of Luckmann's arguments; and critical, and sometimes polemical, discussion of *The Invisible Religion* and its underlying concepts by representatives of competing sociological paradigms.

Since its publication, the perspective Luckmann unfolds in *The Invisible Religion* has not only impacted sociological research and theory on religion, but has also been applied outside sociology in other research fields, such as Egyptology (Assmann 2006).

Hubert Knoblauch is among the scholars who takes up aspects of Luckmann's work, and develops them further, both in terms of empirical application and theoretical refinement. Empirically, a number of Knoblauch's studies (on the non-smoking movement, near-death experiences, the Pope's visit, and other topics; see Knoblauch 2008) are conducted against the backdrop of Luckmann's theory and view of the present state of religion. His concept of "popular religion" (Knoblauch 2012) builds upon Luckmann's idea of new social forms of religion. Knoblauch characterizes much more thoroughly what Luckmann had only outlined as the "new" social form of religion in the last part of this book (chapter 9; see also Soeffner 2017).

Another example of the way in which the perspective of *The Invisible Religion* has been taken up by sociology of religion is Kelly Besecke's study of collective spirituality in the United States (Besecke 2005). Her research is also guided by the question of the contemporary social form of religion. Intending to capture the non-institutional, yet collective, dimension of religion, she proposes a reconceptualization of religion as an evolving social conversation about transcendent meaning. In doing so, she admittedly opposes the identification of non-institutional with private, ultimately intrapsychic religion, which she sees as inherent in Luckmann's treatment of the issue. At the same time, however, she views the transformation of religion addressed by Luckmann as a collective phenomenon, and follows him in locating religion in a communication-based public sphere. Accordingly, she argues for the inclusion of communication about transcendence as a social criterion of secularity, alongside institutional secularity and individual religiosity, suggesting that such communication may have replaced manifest signs of religious meaning in the public sphere in the West.

Key arguments Luckmann put forward in *The Invisible Religion*, as well as its terminology and positioning vis-á-vis other sociological paradigms, have entered into the sociological debate at large as references, guideposts, and to support arguments in contexts not directly treated by Luckmann. In these works, aspects of *The Invisible Religion* are sometimes presented as a warrant, and partly as representative of their school of thought, and the authors select, refer to, or reference the contents of Luckmann's work according to their respective programmatic intentions.

There are a number of related concepts that draw upon key insights from *The Invisible Religion*. For instance, it has found its way into the approach of implicit religion. The concept, as Edward Bailey (1983, 1997) proposes it, focuses on practices within social systems that are not classified as religious (such as economics and politics) as potentially religious. This enables Bailey to assess the extent to which implicitly religious phenomena are a secularized developmental form of specifically Christian practice, or whether they refer to "a globally 'common', a universally 'primordial', a 'paleolithic' but 'perennial' . . . layer of religiosity and humanity" (Bailey 1983: 74). It is in this context that Bailey situates Invisible Religion, for by affirming the latter option, the need arises to take seriously the implicit religion of modern societies if the anthropology of religion is not to remain "confined to the archaic or obsolete" (ibid.). For Bailey, Luckmann's approach is consistent with this research goal. From his own interview research, he provides clues to the contours of contemporary implicit religion. The central element is the Self as an ontological and moral category. In his interpretation of what happens in a British bar, Bailey points to the sacramental function of buying a round of drinks, through which an identity-creating community is created and, above all, situationally stabilized by the associated expectation of reciprocity.

Other concepts such as Roberto Cipriani's *diffused religion* (Cipriani 2003) or Meredith McGuire's *lived religion* (McGuire 2008) owe much to Luckmann's views, as well, and reference *The Invisible Religion* as a paradigmatic treatment of the phenomena they investigate. Instead of detailing these approaches, we want to highlight a case where the fruitful modification of Luckmann's perspective is not limited to qualitative paradigms in sociology of religion. Peter Beyer, in a text on the relationship between church, state, and modernity (Beyer 2000), explores the question of what forms religion, generally, take in modernity. He casts invisible religion as one measurable social form among others. Taking as his starting point the observation that in the political realm the nation still has normative sovereignty over other forms of organization, Beyer asks whether comparable normative priorities also exist in the realm of religion. Contrasting the American confessional and European church models of religion, Beyer identifies fault lines between European and American sociological assessments of these model differences. While American researchers, such as Rodney Stark and Robert Bellah, characterize the weakened institutionalization of the denominational model as a form of religion adapted to modern conditions, Europeans Bryan Wilson and Peter L. Berger see it as diminishing stages within a process of secularization. Luckmann is located by Beyer on the side of the Europeans in this American-European dispute in that he "completes the logic of this [European] stance by also taking into account unformed, namely invisible, religion, and proposing this latter, highly individualistic type as the most representative for the shape of modern religion" (Beyer 2000: 191). Beyer argues that invisible religion, in the sense of a strong anti-institutional individualization, is primarily a European phenomenon, as it functions "as a supplement to the continuing presence of the churches" (ibid.: 196). In the U.S., on the other hand, there is a weakened institutionalized denominational model "with a consistently significant co-presence of invisible religion" (ibid.: 197).

Unsurprisingly, one of the aspects of *The Invisible Religion* that caught the most intense criticism is Luckmann's underlying, very broad definition of religion. Consequently, critical discussion often appears in the context of secularization as the main paradigmatic watershed of sociology of religion. The authors of a survey work on the sociology of religion see Luckmann in the tradition of secularization theory, which they themselves call "The 'Religion' of Secularization" (Christiano et al. 2002: 59). They acknowledge that the idea of invisible religion stands in an "ironic" relationship to secularization theory, "since it could also be seen as a potentially anti-secular argument for the universality of religion. However, by rejecting institutionalized organized religion in general, Luckmann clearly places himself in the secularization camp" (Christiano et al. 2002: 73). Invoking Luckmann's idea that any social process that contributes to the formation of the Self can be called religious, the authors argue that eating with a fork and using toilet paper should be considered religious in this sense, because they transcend the immediate biological nature of humans. While the authors note (seemingly in praise) that this approach saves religion from the "dustbin of history," at the same time it bears little resemblance to what religious and irreligious people today, or ever, would have called religion (Christiano et al. 2002: 75).

Even outside the camp of secularization theorists, Luckmann's concept has been criticized for a supposed lack of applicability. Among the early critics of the concept of invisible religion, Andrew J. Weigert (1974) offered a conceptual critique in this sense. "Luckmann's approach is a theoretical cul de sac for the sociology of religion and may lead to excessive conceptual confusion" (ibid.: 181). Since, according to Weigert, it is axiomatic for Luckmann that human beings are always and everywhere religious insofar as they are human beings, the meaning of more specific questions in the field of empirical research on religion, such as the connection between religion and class, is potentially blurred to the point of meaninglessness. This theory construction leads to problems in empirical application, because it makes it necessary to search for "qualitative themes" that fulfill the identity-creating function on the social and individual level that Luckmann calls religion. Who decides which concrete elements of a worldview or identity are carriers of the function of religion in each society? Since research operating with Luckmann's view already presupposes the religious function of worldview elements, their identification and analysis is never possible independently of the researching observer's position. This, Weigert argues, gives research on invisible religion the character of begging the question (ibid.: 184). Furthermore, there is a threat of *a priori* exclusion of diagnoses that would indicate a loss of meaning of religion, consequently a categorical and pre-empirical denial of secularization. Weigert also opposes the functionalism underlying Luckmann's theory by stating that functions can never be conceived independently of structures or institutions, because "the classification and naming of functions are derived from the structure or carrying institution" (ibid.: 187). According to Weigert, the independence of a "hypostasized" functional sphere leads to the decoupling of sociological analysis from the empirical material, and he sees it as erroneous, as a result of a Luckmannian perspective, to describe, for example, a person who is non-religious in his or her self-definition as religious in the functional sense. Finally, he proposes a transfer of Luckmann's research problem into a sociology of values, whereby values would take over the position of the functional concept of religion, and would have to be examined as manifested in individual and institutional value orientations or identities. Religion would be regarded below the "value sphere" as one among many representatives of such value orientations.

Our cursory remarks sketched above, however, can only begin to describe the enormous fruitfulness and differentiated impact Luckmann's theory of religion has generated, and continues to engender, over the past decades. Even after more than 50 years, the continuing broad international interest in *The Invisible Religion* clearly proves it to be a text that offers strong impulses in multiple directions for critical debate on the forms of contemporary religion, as well as for the ongoing and necessary theoretical and empirical advancement in this area of sociological research. What we have also left largely unaddressed here is the fact that the influence of book goes beyond religion-related academic disciplines and has influenced public discourse. It is precisely one of the outstanding features of *The Invisible Religion* that it has surpassed the narrow limits of academic reasoning and research on religion. It has also been studied by people with a common interest in more general questions regarding culture and society. Many well-informed fellow citizens looking for an accessible, but not superficial or fashionable, description of the fate and prospects of contemporary religion have contributed to its remarkably wide readership. In doing so, it also helped frame public debates about religion in modern society. But that is another topic. The present book provides ample material for what is, in the best sense, an unfinished duty. A comprehensive reconstruction that accounts for its international impact, as well as its critical reappraisal, remain tasks to be accomplished, which exceed the rough classification of the work's influence we have given here. With this expanded new edition of the English version of Thomas Luckmann's work, we want to contribute to continuing and advancing the scholarly discussion of this work, and the subsequent neoclassical turn in the sociology of religion. In doing so, we hope to make a significant contribution that will further advance the sociology of religion as a whole.

Note

1 We thank Robert Glaser for his language editing of this introduction and the translated supplement, and Felix Schwägerl for proofreading the entire book manuscript.

References

Assmann, J. (2006). Invisible Religion and Cultural Memory. In J. Assmann, *Religion and Cultural Memory. Ten Studies* (S. 31–45). Stanford, CA: Stanford University Press (Cultural memory in the present).

Bailey, E. (1983). The Implicit Religion of Contemporary Society. An Orientation and Plea for Its Study. *Religion* 13(1), S. 69–83. DOI: 10.1016/0048–721X(83)90006–4.

Bailey, E. (1997). *Implicit Religion in Contemporary Society*. Kampen, Weinheim: Kok Pharos Publ. House (Theologie und Empirie, 28).

Berger, P. L. (1990). *The Sacred Canopy. Elements of a Sociological Theory of Religion*. New York: Doubleday.

Berger, P. L., & Luckmann, T. (1967). *The Social Construction of Reality. A Treatise in the Sociology of Knowledge*. Anchor books ed. Garden City, NY: Doubleday (Anchor books, A 589).

Berger, P. L., & Luckmann, T. (1995). *Modernity, Pluralism and the Crisis of Meaning. The Orientation of Modern Man*. Gütersloh: Bertelsmann Foundation Publ.

Besecke, K. (2005). Seeing Invisible Religion: Religion as a Societal Conversation About Transcendent Meaning. *Sociological Theory* 23(2), S. 179–196. DOI: 10.1111/j.0735–2751.2005.00249.x.

Beyer, P. (2000). Modern Forms of the Religious Life. Denomination, Church, and Invisible Religion in Canada, the United States, and Europe. In *Rethinking Church, State, and Modernity. Canada Between Europe and America* (S. 189–210). Toronto: University of Toronto Press.

Christiano, K. J., Swatos, W. H., & Kivisto, P. (2002). *Sociology of Religion. Contemporary Developments*. Walnut Creek: AltaMira Press.

Cipriani, R. (2003). Invisible Religion or Diffused Religion in Italy? *Social Compass* 50(3), S. 311–320. DOI: 10.1177/00377686030503005.

Durkheim, É. (2008). *The Elementary Forms of Religious Life*. Oxford: Oxford University Press (Oxford world's classics).

Husserl, E. (2005). *Logical Investigations*. Reprinted. London: Routledge & Kegan Paul (International library of philosophy).

Knoblauch, H. (2008). Spirituality and Popular Religion in Europe. *Social Compass* 55(2), S. 140–153. DOI: 10.1177/0037768607089735.

Knoblauch, H. (2012). Popular Religion. In *Encyclopedia of Global Religion* (S. 1007–1009). Thousand Oaks, CA: SAGE Reference.

Luckmann, T. (1956). *A Comparative Study of Four Protestant Parishes in Germany*. PhD Thesis, New School for Social Research, New York, Graduate Faculty.

Luckmann, T. (1957). The Evangelical Academies. An Experiment in German Protestantism. *Christianity and Crisis* 17(4), S. 68–70.

Luckmann, T. (1959). Four Protestant Parishes in Germany. A Study in the Sociology of Religion. *Social Research* 26, S. 423–448.

Luckmann, T. (1960). Neuere Schriften zur Religionssoziologie. *Kölner Zeitschrift für Soziologie und Sozialpsychologie* 12(2), S. 315–326.

Luckmann, T. (1963a). *Das Problem der Religion in der modernen Gesellschaft. Institution, Person und Weltanschauung*. Freiburg im Breisgau: Rombach.

Luckmann, T. (1963b). On Religion in Modern Society. Individual Consciousness, World View, Institution. *Journal for the Scientific Study of Religion* 2(2), S. 147–162.

Luckmann, T. (1983). Secularization – A Contemporary Myth. In T. Luckmann, *Life-World and Social Realities* (S. 124–132). London: Heinemann.

Luckmann, T. (1991). *Die unsichtbare Religion*. Frankfurt am Main: Suhrkamp (Suhrkamp-Taschenbuch Wissenschaft, 947).

McGuire, M. B. (2008). *Lived Religion. Faith and Practice in Everyday Life*. Oxford: Oxford University Press Incorporated. Available online: https://ebookcentral.proquest.com/lib/kxp/detail.action?docID=665414.

Mead, G. H. (2015). *Mind, Self, and Society*. Chicago, London: The University of Chicago Press.

Plessner, H. (2019). *Levels of Organic Life and the Human. An Introduction to Philosophical Anthropology*. First ed. New York: Fordham University Press (Forms of living).

Schutz, A. (1972a). On Multiple Realities. In A. Schutz und M. Natanson, *Collected Papers I, Bd. 11* (S. 207–259). Dordrecht: Springer Netherlands (Phaenomenologica).

Schutz, A. (1972b). *The Phenomenology of the Social World*. 1st paperback ed. Evanston, IL: Northwestern University Press (Northwestern University studies in phenomenology & existential philosophy).

Soeffner, H.-G. (2017). *The Order of Rituals. The Interpretation of Everyday Life*. Milton Park: Routledge.

Wagner, F. (1991). *Was ist Religion? Studien zu ihrem Begriff und Thema in Geschichte und Gegenwart. 2. Aufl.* Gütersloh: Mohn.

Weber, M. (2012). The "Objectivity" of Knowledge in Social Science and Social Policy. In H. H. Bruun und S. Whimster, *Max Weber. Complete Methodological Writings* (S. 100–138). London: Routledge (Weber in translation).

Weigert, A. J. (1974). Whose Invisible Religion? Luckmann Revisited. *Sociological Analysis* 35(3), S. 181–188. DOI: 10.2307/3710648.

Wohlrab-Sahr, M. (2000). Was Has Happened Since "Luckmann 1960"? *Sociology of Religion in Germany, Austria, and Switzerland* 26(1). DOI: 10.5169/seals-814791.

Thomas Luckmann

The Invisible Religion

As there thus seems to be no one elementary religious emotion, but only a common storehouse of emotion upon which religious objects may draw, so there might conceivably also prove to be no one specific and essential kind of religious object, and no one specific and essential kind of religious act.

William James
The Varieties of Religious Experience

FOREWORD

This essay was originally motivated by my dissatisfaction with the limitations of various empirical studies in the sociology of religion – my own included. The problems developed in the present essay were first touched upon in my review of some publications in the sociology of religion, published in the *Kölner Zeitschrift für Soziologie und Sozialpsychologie* (12:2, 1960, pp. 315–326). Later I wrote a first draft of the present essay under the title "Notes on the Case of the Missing Religion" which, if for no other reason, remained unpublished because of its title. Arnold Bergstraesser, late professor of political science and sociology at the University of Freiburg, encouraged me to rewrite the draft and publish it in German in the Sociological Series edited by him for Rombach Freiburg. The volume was published in 1963 under the title *Das Problem der Religion in der modernen Gesellschaft.*

In 1962 I read a paper on the problem of religion in modern society to the annual meeting of the Society for the Scientific Study of Religion. The paper was published in the Society's *Journal* (2: 12, 1963, pp. 147–162). Having undertaken to translate – or retranslate – the volume published by Rombach for American publication, I found myself rewriting it. Some sections were expanded, others reformulated, still others shortened.

In addition to the late Arnold Bergstraesser I am indebted to my teacher in the sociology of religion, Carl Mayer of the Graduate Faculty of the New School for Social Research, New York, Peter Berger of the Graduate Center of the City University of New York, and Friedrich Tenbruck of the University of Frankfurt for many fruitful discussions of the problems treated in the present volume.

INTRODUCTION*

In our day the autonomy of individual existence appears to have become problematic. One of the reasons for this is the fear that highly organized, monolithic society is suppressing many areas in which individuality might otherwise have free play. The social sciences need not take such fear at face value – but they cannot ignore the possibility that it is the symptom of a genuine problem. Although the social sciences have come to concern themselves almost exclusively with the analysis of social "systems," they must not treat the fate of the individual in society as irrelevant. The perennial question as to how man is located in the social order can be today most cogently articulated in the social sciences. In various metamorphoses, that question, inherited from philosophy, reappears in the different branches of the social sciences. The problem of the relation of constraint and freedom, order and anarchy runs like a thread through classical sociology. It also constitutes the fundamental question of the theory of social institutions, social change, and the theory of individual socialization. It is linked to the problems of role theory and the anthropological study of culture and personality. Its central place in political science is obvious, but it is also, less obviously, involved in the discussion of some basic axioms of economic theory. Whereas the problem cannot be resolved, indeed, not even fully articulated, within a single discipline, it is clearly a problem that directly or indirectly must concern all the social sciences.

The problem claims attention with renewed urgency today. What is the impact of modern society upon the course of individual life? In what way can a person

* Editorial note: In the 1967 version, all references are listed in endnotes. We have carefully edited this and included all footnotes that only contain literature references in the text. The book's bibliography can be found at the end in a complete listing on p. 102. The bibliographical references to the Supplement are listed separately on p. 119.

DOI: 10.4324/9781003257875-1

maintain his autonomy in this society? In addition to its relevance to theory in the social sciences, the problem – as such questions indicate – carries concrete and pressing implications for contemporary man.

It must be admitted that the schools of thought dominant in recent sociology were reluctant to take up this problem. The terms "individualism" and "mass society" have been bandied about by various "social critics" so much that they have lost all meaning. Their use was so often linked to fundamentally romantic views of traditional society that they necessarily appeared suspect to a discipline which prided itself upon its recently acquired value-freedom. Much of the literary controversy that raged on the problems of "mass society" and "individualism" remained, therefore, outside the precincts of academic social science. But the general resonance of that controversy, and the serious reflections on contemporary life that it occasioned, imparted even to the more ascetic sociologists the suspicion that the substance of the controversy might be, after all, somewhat more than trivial.

On cursory inspection one could perhaps regard the problem as one version of the general sociological problem of socialization, injected – unnecessarily – with a certain amount of topical sensationalism by the "social critics" and other contemporary Cassandras. Reasoning along such lines, one might yet concede that the processes of socialization in modern society have become less coherent than they had been in traditional societies. Rapid social change, increasing social mobility, transformations in the structure of the family, and the high level of rational organization of various social institutions – so one might argue – tend to produce certain difficulties in individual adaptation to the social order. Such difficulties could very well appear dramatic to the individual who, in addition, would find support for the subjective illusion that his problems are historically unique in the literary condemnations of "mass society." Yet – so runs the argument further – all this does not require a *theoretical* reorientation. Reasoning along such or similar lines, the most important movement in contemporary sociology, structural-functionalism, considers the problem in question as resolved in principle while admitting that further study of empirical details might be necessary.

Let us now consider another possibility. What if the relation of the individual to the social order underwent a radical transformation with the emergence of modern society? In that case sociology would be confronted with a problem which could not be resolved by simple application of the "universal" structural-functional theories of socialization and social change. The theory of socialization posits generally identical processes of internalization of cultural "contents" in a given "social system." It is predicated upon an ahistorical conception of the relation between "social" and "psychological systems." The theory of social change explains specific institutional changes by reference to a functional model of equilibrium within the "social system." Starting out from a dialectic conception of the relation between individual and society in history, however, one must be ready to inspect the hypothesis that a fundamental shift occurred in the "location" of the individual in the social order in modern society. If the *possibility* of such a shift is granted, the discussions about the effect of "mass society" upon "individualism" appear in a new light. They may be interpreted as symptoms of the relocation of the individual in the social order. If there are qualitatively different patterns of location of the individual in society and if institutional change may lead to qualitatively different forms of society, an ahistorical conception of socialization and institutional change no longer appears adequate and a new theoretical effort is required of sociology.

We shall try to contribute to this effort in the present essay. No "social critical" intent – as expressed, for example, in the current use of a term such as "mass society" – underlies this attempt. Starting out from the assumption that the relation between individual existence and the social order is historical, we admit, however, our belief that the problem of individual existence in society has reached a critical point in the contemporary world. If the sociologist wishes his theories to remain relevant for his fellow men he must not refuse to raise the questions that agitate them, in the context of scientific discourse. It can be said of most brands of "social criticism" that – while seeing the problem – they failed to formulate it dispassionately and in a manner which permits the inspection of evidence. This, we take it, is one of the most important tasks for the sociologist.

A unifying perspective on the problem of individual existence in society is to be found in the sociological theory of religion. This insight must be attributed, within the sociological tradition, to Émile Durkheim and Max Weber. Both were profoundly interested in the fate of the individual in modern society. Both recognized that the character of modern society carried serious consequences for the individual. Their studies of the division of labor, bureaucratization, suicide, and so forth are characterized by this interest. No matter that their methodologies were value-free – the grave concern for the social conditions of individual existence in the contemporary world clearly expresses the moral engagement of their sociological theorizing. Different as their theories are, it is remarkable that both Weber and Durkheim sought the key to an understanding of the social location of the individual in the study of religion. For Durkheim, the symbolic reality of religion is the core of the *conscience collective*. As social fact, it transcends the individual and is the condition for social integration and the continuity of the social order. At the same time, only the internalization of that objective reality by the subject makes man into a social and, thereby, a moral and genuinely human being. For Durkheim man is essentially *homo duplex* and individuation has, necessarily, a social basis. The problem with which we are concerned here is seen by Durkheim in a universal anthropological perspective and is articulated by him, correspondingly, in a radical manner. For Weber, on the other hand, the problem of the social conditions of individuation appears in a more specific perspective – that is, in the historical context of particular religions and their relation to historical societies. When it came to the question of the individual in modern society, however, both Weber and Durkheim linked it directly to the secularization of the contemporary world. It can be said that both Weber and Durkheim recognized what is presupposed in the present essay: that the problem of individual existence in society is a "religious" problem. We maintain, then, that the relevance of sociology for contemporary man derives primarily from its search for an understanding of the fate of the person in the structure of modern society. The sociologist today need look no farther than the "classical" traditions of his own discipline to find illumination in this search if – as we think – the convergence in the thinking of Durkheim and Weber on the point discussed earlier merits to be taken as a more important heritage for contemporary sociology than the methodological and theoretical controversies on "historicism," "functionalism," "*Verstehen*," the ontological status of social facts, and so forth.

1

RELIGION, CHURCH, AND SOCIOLOGY

One might be justified in looking to the sociology of religion as the most likely branch of sociology to have brought the problem which concerns us here into sharp focus. Little more was needed than to articulate the theoretical convergence of Durkheim and Weber, which we pointed out in the preceding remarks, to derive from it hypotheses about the "religious" components of the relation of individuals to contemporary societies and to proceed to verify or refute them by empirical research. Scrutinizing the publications in the recent sociology of religion, one finds, indeed, a rapidly increasing number of studies in parish sociology, the demography of the churches, statistics of participation in church activities, many analyses of sectarian movements, some monographs of ecclesiastic organizations and, based upon the strategies of opinion research, various studies of religious "beliefs." The sociology of religion today is a flourishing enterprise, characterized not only by large quantities of studies but also by a proliferation of specialized journals, conferences, symposia, and institutes. Present-day sociology of religion can be easily compared – in personnel, financing, and production – to the most fashionable and best-endowed branches in the social sciences and sociology. This is all the more remarkable in view of the fact that it is all due to a very recent development, beginning after the Second World War and accelerating in the last decade (cf. Luckmann 1960: 315–326).

Unfortunately, one is disappointed in trying to find theoretical significance in the recent sociology of religion. The external flourishing of the discipline was not accompanied by theoretical progress. On the contrary, compared to Weber's and Durkheim's view of religion as the key to the understanding of society, the state of theory in the recent sociology of religion is, in the main, regressive. The classical positions were largely abandoned and the sociology of religion became increasingly narrow and trivial. Its links with Durkheim's and Weber's sociologies

DOI: 10.4324/9781003257875-2

of religion are, at best, superficial. The awareness of the central significance of religion for sociological theory was lost – in the sociology of religion as much as in the other branches of sociology. The new sociology of religion consists mainly of descriptions of the decline of ecclesiastic institutions – from a parochial viewpoint, at that. The definition of research problems and programs is, typically, determined by the institutional forms of traditional church organization. The new sociology of religion badly neglected its theoretically most significant task: to analyze the changing social – not necessarily institutional – basis of religion in modern society. In developing the thesis that, for sociological theory, the problem of personal existence in society is essentially a question of the social form of religion, we can count on little direct help from the new sociology of religion. A beginning can be made, however, by a critical examination of the theoretical assumptions and by an interpretation of the findings of that discipline.

At first, it appears paradoxical that the apparent flourishing of the sociology of religion in recent decades was paralleled by a decline of its theoretical significance. The paradox resolves itself if one considers the major economic, ideological, and institutional causes which led to this illusory renaissance. After the "classical" period of sociological interest in religion the center of gravity in the sociological enterprise shifted to America. Religion was increasingly considered under the perspectives of social evolutionism – to wit, a form of historical reductionism – or under the perspectives of psychological reductionism represented by behaviorism and positivism. Religion no longer occupied an important place in sociological theory. The few social scientists who were concerned with the study of religion were cultural anthropologists. Even they tended to view the importance of religion in the context of primitive and traditional societies and failed, on the whole, to recognize its implications for general sociological theory.

Inasmuch as interest in the "classical" sociology of religion was preserved, it tended to be predominantly historical and exegetic. Max Weber's sociology of religion was understood as a grandiose exercise in historical sociology, whereas its role in Weber's general theory of society was largely neglected. Analogously, Durkheim's sociology of religion was interpreted, in the main, as a sociologistic theory of the origin of religion; having narrowed down its relevance to primitive society, the theory was disputed for its ethnological deficiencies. It is not surprising that the points of kinship between Weber and Durkheim were disregarded. Sociology in Europe was characterized by an almost complete lack of communication between the French and the German tradition of sociological theory. But even from the more detached vantage point of American sociology, the congruence of Durkheim's and Weber's sociologies of religion was generally overlooked. Only Talcott Parsons recognized this congruence (cf. Parsons 1949: 52–66, 163). But Parsons – whose great merit it was to introduce both Durkheim and Weber into the mainstream of American sociology – failed to exploit adequately the theoretical possibilities which resulted from that convergence. This may be attributed, perhaps, to the fact that he was mainly interested in incorporating Durkheim's "functionalist" conception of religious representations and Weber's institutional theory into his own structuralfunctional system of theory, in which religion occupies a circumscribed place as an institutional subsystem with special integrating functions.

More astounding is the complete failure, in American sociology, to recognize the possibilities inherent in both Durkheim's conception of *homo duplex* and George H. Mead's theory of the social origin of Self. Both theories are characterized by a complete reversal of the traditional understanding of the relation between society and individual. Whereas the individual had been generally viewed as something that is indubitably given, combining with others to form "society" – the explanatory principle for that combination being contract, power, social "instinct," and so forth – both Durkheim and Mead posit society as given, either as "fact" or "process," and find in it the necessary condition for individuation and the emergence of Self, respectively. The radical character of this reversal and its implications for sociological theory were often overlooked; its significance for an understanding of the relation between society, religion, and person is yet to be articulated.

The thirties and forties were lean years for the sociology of religion. A whole generation of sociologists grew up in an intellectual climate in which religion was regarded as a system of beliefs which had performed certain integrating functions in primitive society, if not as a prehistoric stage in the evolution of human reason, whose institutional survival in contemporary society offered little research interest to the sociologist.

But then, in the postwar years, sociology was "discovered" by the churches. Increasingly, it exerted a strange fascination for church administrators and ecclesiastic organization men, as well as for some pastoral theologians, professors of social ethics, and the like. Sufficiently large numbers of sociologists responded to staff the research undertakings created by this interest. In consequence, the sociology of religion was reborn, but, basically, as an applied or ancillary science. Its problems were defined by the institutional interest of religious organizations. Most studies were geared to the requirements of the sponsors, but even in those studies which were technically independent the pragmatic restrictions of research interest inspired by the alliance between church organizations and sociologists were generally taken for granted.

Another consequence of this alliance was a strong tendency toward denominational sociologies of religion. This was especially true of Europe where a Catholic and, to a lesser extent, a Protestant sociology of religion has been brought into existence. In the United States, the tendency toward Catholic, Protestant, and Jewish sociologies of religion is less pronounced, but even here it is by no means negligible. It must be admitted, of course, that a division of labor along denominational lines may be a useful thing in the study of historically differentiated religious institutions. At the same time, interdenominational conferences and the presence of some "independent" sociologists of religion notwithstanding, the situation fostered a parochial outlook in research. This is all the more serious in view of the minimal development of systematic theory in the sociology of religion. For one thing, it is rather difficult to compare and to interpret the results of research whose problems are largely defined along denominational lines.

The demand for usable research results on the part of church institutions and the absence of theory also had consequences for the methodology of the new sociology of religion. The exclusion of matters of "faith" from research, the pragmatic orientation of most research and the absence of theory in the definition of problems combined to encourage the adoption of research techniques which were "handy" – but not necessarily appropriate to the study of religion. Thus, for example, methods of institutional description were transferred to the analysis of church organization in a rather naïve fashion. Even more characteristic, however, of the new sociology of religion was its uncritical, on occasion primitive, use of opinion research techniques. Interestingly enough, there is hardly another sociological discipline as completely dominated by a narrow "positivistic" methodology as the recent sociology of religion.

It must be added, however, that with these remarks, we are referring to the sociology of religion in the technical sense of the term. The history of religion continued to follow paths that had been set by the historical and theological traditions of the nineteenth century. Furthermore, in France as well as, perhaps to a smaller degree, in the United States, the work of Durkheim and his school never completely ceased to influence cultural anthropology. We need not enter into a detailed description of these developments here. It may suffice to refer to the works of Rudolf Otto, G. van der Leeuw, Mircea Eliade, Roger Caillois, Joachim Wach, W. Lloyd Warner, and others whose historical and anthropological studies of religion offer proof that these disciplines did not join the trend toward triviality which marks the recent sociology of religion. On the other hand, historical and ethnological analyses of religion are not yet equivalent to a systematic sociology theory of religion. This must be said despite the fact that these disciplines contributed valuable empirical material as well as important beginnings of theory. The discovery of constants in primitive mythology, based on comparative studies, the phenomenology of religious experience and so forth, are valuable steps toward a sociological theory of religion. Their usefulness is severely diminished, however, by the absence of social-structural analyses; a fact which encourages either historicist or psychologistic misinterpretations in such studies.

Returning to the recent sociology of religion, we may say that it is theoretically inadequate. In the absence of systematic theory, a body of tacit assumptions developed which perform the function of theory. These assumptions are fairly uniform; a fact that is all the more surprising since they emerged in a discipline which tends toward "denominationalism," which still maintains a national rather than international character and in which research is marked by very different degrees of technical competence. Although these tacit assumptions perform the function of systematic theory, it can hardly be maintained that they do so legitimately. The fear is not unjustified that they have crystallized into a scientific ideology which hinders an unprejudiced view on the problem of religion in modern society. It will serve the purposes of our analysis to articulate these assumptions.

The main assumption – which also has the most important consequences for research and theory in the sociology of religion – consists in the identification of church and religion. On occasion, this assumption is explicitly formulated as a methodological principle: religion may be many things, but it is amenable to scientific analysis only to the extent that it becomes organized and institutionalized. Most other assumptions are intimately linked with this main assumption or directly derived from it. Religion becomes a social fact either as ritual (institutionalized religious conduct) or doctrine (institutionalized religious ideas). Frequently, it is assumed that, on the part of the individual, religious "needs" correspond to the objective social facts of religion – which latter satisfy the former in some manner. It is then left open whether the historical varieties of religious institutions such as churches and sects satisfy somewhat different individual "needs," whether socio-historic circumstances account for different organizational forms, whether "religion" is the sum of all of these, or whether it is their common denominator.

The identification of church and religion fits into the dominant view of sociology as the science of social institutions – the latter term understood narrowly. It is also congruent with theoretical positivism. In the traditional positivistic view, religion is the institutional conglomerate of certain irrational beliefs. These are assumed to result from the confrontation of individuals and societies with a cognitively not yet manageable reality. It is well known that the original positivistic position contained the thesis that religion, as a primitive stage in the evolution of human reason, would be eventually replaced by science.

Vestiges of this view have entered the understanding – or misunderstanding – of secularization that characterizes much of the recent sociology of religion. In the absence of a well-founded theory, secularization is typically regarded as a process of religious pathology to be measured by the shrinking reach of the churches. Since the institutional vacuum is not being filled by a counter-church – which was still envisaged by Comte – one readily concludes that modern society is nonreligious. It matters little that the process is evaluated negatively by those sociologists of religion who have inner or professional commitments to the churches; their model of interpretation is borrowed from the positivistic thesis. The churches remain, in a manner of speaking, islands of religion (or irrationality) in a sea of secularism (or reason). It only remains for the sociologist of religion to analyze the national and class differences in the process of religious decline – that is, of the shrinking reach of the churches. Under these circumstances, it need surprise no one that the historical and ethnological horizons of the recent sociology of religion are, on the whole, extremely narrow.

Such a view of secularization, derived from the dominant sociological view of religion, is consistent with the theories of the increasing specialization of institutions and institutional areas in modern society. Religious institutions, too, are taken to have an increasingly specialized function in modern society. The observable changes in the structure of religious institutions tend to be explained by transformations in other areas of the social system. The reasons for the shrinking reach of the churches are sought in the processes of urbanization and industrialization which – so runs the argument – "undermined" other traditional institutions also. Only if the identity of church and religion is postulated can it be overlooked that this explanation begs the question. It is important to note that the identification of church and religion – whatever historical and sociological reasons there may be for it – cannot be but entirely acceptable to the churches. An institutional interpretation of religion is close to the manner in which the churches generally understood themselves, the theological arguments over the visible and the invisible church notwithstanding. A functionalist view of institutionalized religion, moreover, could be regarded as a welcome, if unintended, support for institutional claims to religious monopoly – if demonstrably inapplicable for the present, then at least providing theoretical support for a romantic view of the past.

An indirect and incidental advantage of the identification of church and religion is that it legitimates the transfer of the techniques of institutional analysis to the study of religion, obviating methodological reflection on the special nature of the problem. An important consequence of this situation is the concentration of research upon the parishes and congregations. It follows from the assumption that the administrative organization of the churches predefines the areas in which religion can become a tangible social fact. In any case, the bulk of the recent sociology of religion is parish sociology.

The assumption that church and religion are identical is accompanied by certain ideas about individual religiosity. The latter is typically taken as being based upon psychological "needs" which are decisively structured by the specialized religious institutions – to wit, the church – and "satisfied" by them. In this assumption, a number of different axioms of psychological and sociology functionalism are confused. Although this confusion is not restricted to the sociology of religion, it has especially serious consequences for it. It provides a highly inadequate scheme for the understanding of the relation between individual, religion, and society. Certainly individual religiosity cannot be understood without reference to a given historical and institutional reality of ritual and belief. It may be assumed that this reality offers itself, as it were, for subjective internalization. Recognition of the historical character of socialization, however, is incompatible with the assumption of religious "needs" and cannot justify an identification of religiosity and church-oriented religiosity. It is a dubious procedure to attach to a complex social-psychological phenomenon a label such as "need" which, at best, has its place in the analytic model of a hypothetical *homo psychologicus*.

We must repeat that the assumptions we are discussing generally do not form an explicit body of axioms. They do combine in an orientation which underlies a large portion of research in the recent sociology of religion. This orientation manifests itself in the definition of research problems, in guidelines of research procedure and, occasionally, in the *ad hoc* "theories" by which the findings are interpreted. The distinction between an "objective" and a "subjective" dimension of religiosity plays an important role, both for methodology and *ad hoc* "theories." As a rule, the "objective" dimension is identified with "observable" behavior. In practice, this leads to an operational definition of the "objective" dimension of religiosity as institutional participation. The most cherished statistics of parish sociology are church attendance percentages. Church attendance is, of course, an important form of social action if one is to study churchoriented religiosity. The difficulties start only if one posits a simple relationship between the "objective" fulfillment of an institutionally defined norm and the social-psychological phenomenon of church-oriented religiosity in its subjective totality. The difficulties are compounded by the all too frequent reliance upon attendance figures while other – incidentally also more or less "measurable" – components of church-oriented religiosity are neglected; if, in other words, church attendance indices are taken as a master index for church-oriented religiosity. Finally, it is entirely impermissible to base interpretations of the presence or absence of religion *tout court* upon such statistics, a temptation which not all studies in the recent sociology of religion were able to resist successfully.

The "subjective" dimension of religiosity is usually identified with religious opinions or attitudes. Consequently, standard techniques of opinion research are used in the study of religiosity without much doubt as to their adequacy. In a few instances, technically more advanced techniques of attitude research have been used, but especially in Europe, the majority of empirical studies in the recent sociology of religion were less than sophisticated in their research methodology. Institutionally defined doctrines and theological positions are the subject of questions in interviews or of items in questionnaires. Respondents may then either agree or disagree, or on occasion, locate themselves upon a scale. Religiosity is sometimes defined, for research purposes, even more naïvely, as being "for" or "against" a given church, denomination, and so forth. All too easily the identification of church with religion leads first to operational shortcuts to religion, via segregated opinion items on doctrinal matters, via "quantified" affective loads with respect to an ecclesiastic organization and the like.

We need not go into further details in this characterization of the recent sociology of religion. What was already said serves to illustrate the reasons for the predominantly trivial character of this discipline. Needless to say, this brief description does not do justice to some of the theoretically more advanced and technically competent work in the sociology of religion. Admittedly, the description had a polemic intention. Yet it is hardly exaggerated if one reviews the field as a whole. It is fair to say that at present the sociology of religion is divorced from the main issues of social theory. The assumptions underlying most research are based upon an identification of religion with its prevalent, fully institutionalized form. The discipline, thereby, accepts the self-interpretations – and the ideology – of religious institutions as valid definitions of the range of their subject matter. Most, if not all, research accepts a methodology which imported techniques from other fields and which dictates restriction to the tabulation of overt institutionalized performances and the scoring of atomistically defined opinion items.

It must be obvious that the new sociology of religion is exclusively concerned with church-oriented religiosity. One may wonder whether it possesses the theoretical and methodological resources to analyze and interpret adequately even that phenomenon. This, however, is a question which is of subordinate importance compared to the fact that the discipline completely neglects the central question of the sociology of religion which is, at the same time, an important problem for sociological theory as a whole: What are the conditions under which "transcendent," superordinated, and "integrating" structures of meaning are socially objectivated? No doubt the churches, as specialized religious institutions, deserve to be carefully studied by sociologists. In addition, there is little reason to object to applied and sponsored research merely because it may be trivial from a theoretical point of view. It is regrettable, however, that the recent sociology of religion as a whole failed to continue the traditions of the classical sociology of religion and, in consequence, acquired the character of a rather narrowly conceived sociography of the churches. Once the sociology of religion uncritically takes it for granted that church and religion are identical, it blinds itself to its most relevant problem. It has prejudged the answer to the question whether, in contemporary society, any socially objectivated meaning structures but the traditional institutionalized religious doctrines function to integrate the routines of everyday life and to legitimate its crises. It therefore fails to concern itself with the most important, essentially religious, aspects of the location of the individual in society.

II

CHURCH-ORIENTED RELIGION ON THE PERIPHERY OF MODERN SOCIETY

While our appraisal of the recent sociology of religion could not but turn critical, it was not undertaken for the sake of criticism. It served to demonstrate, rather, that the inability of the recent sociology of religion to provide an account of the place of religion in modern industrial society was to be attributed partly to the theoretical impoverishment, and partly to the methodological shortcomings, of that discipline. It would be wrong, however, to take this criticism as an invitation to declare the recent sociology of religion as incompetent, irrelevant, and immaterial. It is true that church-oriented religion is merely one and perhaps not even the most important element in the situation that characterizes religion in modern society. In the absence of adequate research on that situation, *in toto*, it would be foolish to disregard the abundant data which recent research in the sociology of religion did provide on church-oriented religion in contemporary industrial societies. No attempt to theorize about religion in modern society can afford the luxury of leaving aside the material so assiduously collected – even if, as we suggested, it may fail to tell the whole story. It is reasonable, therefore, that we begin with a summary review and interpretation of that material.

During the past decades, and especially in the last ten years, many studies of churches, sects, and denominations accumulated. Most studies originated in the United States, Germany, France, Belgium, England, and the Netherlands, with a few coming from other countries such as Italy and Austria. In the European countries research concentrated, with a few exceptions, on Catholicism and the established or quasi-established Protestant churches. In the United States, the sects received the major share of attention, although Judaism, Catholicism, and the major Protestant denominations were not completely neglected.[1]

DOI: 10.4324/9781003257875-3

Despite the large number of studies, it is not without difficulty that one may proceed to generalizations about the location of church-oriented religion in modern industrial society. With some exaggeration, one may venture the remark that the wealth of data – in the absence of a common theoretical framework – proves to be more of an embarrassment than an advantage. Since most studies have concentrated on sociographic details, it is easier to discern the local, regional, national, and doctrinal peculiarities of the churches than the common social characteristics of church-oriented religion. To add to the difficulties, some authors have ecclesiastic, if not theological commitments. It is, therefore, sometimes necessary to disentangle the data from a certain bias in interpretation. The fact that we cannot present all findings in detail here compounds the difficulties. If we are to gain an overall picture of church-oriented religion in modern society as a first step toward an understanding of religion in the contemporary world, we must face the risk of some oversimplification. In order to minimize this risk, we shall present only such generalizations as are based on convergent rather than on isolated findings. Even after taking this precaution, it is to be admitted that the generalizations cannot be taken as proven beyond all doubt. They are, however, conclusions favored by the weight of available evidence.[2]

In Europe it is common knowledge that the country is more "religious" than the city. This is generally borne out by the findings of research in the sociology of religion. From church attendance figures to religious burial reports, various statistics which can be taken as indicative of church-oriented religion show consistently higher averages for rural than for urban areas. On the basis of such statistics, only a small proportion of the urban population can be described as church-oriented. It is of some interest to note, however, that there is a long-range trend toward a decrease of church-oriented religion in rural regions too. Consequently, the difference in church-oriented religion, while not completely leveled, is smaller now than several decades ago. It hardly needs to be added that this is merely part of a more general process. The transformations in the distribution of church-oriented religion are linked to increasing economic interpenetration of city and country, the growing rationalization of farming, the diffusion of urban culture to the country through mass media, and so forth. It should be noted, however, that these transformations do not proceed at an even rate. In addition to local and regional circumstances of economic and political character the specifically "religious" historical tradition of a region or congregation may speed up or retard the process.

According to another item of common knowledge, women are more "religious" than men and the young and old more "religious" than other age groups. Research findings indicate that such opinions need to be revised at least in part. Indeed, women generally do better than men on various indices of church-oriented religion, and the middle generation is, in fact, characterized by lower participation and attendance rates than the young and the old.

It is significant, however, that working women as a category tend to resemble men more closely in church orientation than, for example, housewives do. This hardly supports the view that women, children, and old people have something like a natural inclination for church-oriented religion. The findings represent an important aspect of the social distribution of church-oriented religion rather than being indicative of the psychology of sex and age. In general terms, we may say, that the degree of involvement in the work processes of modern industrial society correlates negatively with the degree of involvement in church-oriented religion. It is obvious, of course, that the degree of involvement in such processes is in turn linked with age- and sex-roles.

The involvement of the working population in church-oriented religion – while lower than that of the rest of the population – is, however, itself significantly differentiated. Among the various occupational groups can be found important differences in participation. The indices are generally higher for agricultural, white-collar, and some professional groups. These differences coincide roughly with the distribution of church-oriented religion among social classes. Farmers, peasants, and those elements of the middle classes which are basically survivals of the traditional bourgeoisie and petite bourgeoisie are marked by a degree of involvement in church-oriented religion which is disproportionately higher than that of the working class.

In addition to church attendance, opinions on doctrinal matters and so forth, some recent studies in the sociology of religion also investigated participation in various nonritual activities of the churches, ranging from youth clubs to charitable enterprises. These studies indicate that in Europe, only a small fraction of the members of congregations join activities that lie outside of the ritual functions of the churches. While those participating in these functions – whom we may collectively call the ritual core of the congregation – represent only a relatively small part of the nominal membership of the parish, they are yet more numerous than those otherwise active in the church. The size of that latter group, the hard core of active members, varies from region to region and from one denomination to the other. It can be said that the major factors determining these differences are the ecology of the community and the distribution of social classes and occupational groups within the parish. The role which these factors play in the selection of the "hard core" from the congregational membership as a whole, however, is not as important as the role these same factors play in the initial recruitment of the congregation from the reservoir of merely nominal members. While some aspects of the relation between society and churchoriented religion are common knowledge, there can be little doubt that for the industrial countries of Western Europe the findings of the recent sociology of religion describe this relation with more precision. They establish a clear connection between the distribution of church-oriented religion and a number of demographic and other sociologically relevant variables. In the foregoing, we described the most important of these. We must, however, draw attention to the fact that the figures vary from country to country and from denomination to denomination. By most criteria, Catholicism exhibits higher rates of participation than Protestantism. Some part of this variation can be attributed to differences in the degree of industrialization characterizing Catholic and Protestant countries, respectively, to the presence or absence of a tradition of militant socialism, to different forms of church-state relations and other factors. At the same time, there are considerable national and regional differences which cannot be attributed directly to demographic, economic, or political factors. The level of participation in church-oriented religion seems to be exceptionally low in the case of Anglicanism. Or, to refer to another example, there are differences in the level of participation among French Catholic dioceses which can be attributed in part to sociologically rather intangible historical traditions. Note should be taken also of another factor, neglected in our present summary, that seems to be involved in the distribution of church-oriented religion: the proportion of the members of a denomination in the total population. With certain exceptions, so-called diaspora congregations are characterized by relatively high attendance and participation figures.

These remarks should not obscure the overriding influence of economic, political, and class variables in determining the distribution of church-oriented religion in present-day Western Europe. Before we proceed to draw conclusions about religion in modern society, the European data must be compared with the findings of research on religion in the United States.

For several reasons, such a comparison is difficult. First, the great variety of institutional expressions of religion in America has not yet been thoroughly and systematically investigated, although at least the major and most typical expressions and some of the sects, fascinating to the sociologist for one reason or another, did receive attention. Second, among the studies that were carried out, some were guided by a pronounced positivistic bias. The third and most important reason is the unique social and religious history of America. For this, more than for any other reason, caution is indicated in summary characterizations of church religion in America, especially if they are to be used for comparison with the European findings. A sizable number of processes and circumstances find no close parallel in European social history; for example, the absence of a feudal past and of a peasantry, the peculiar complex of conditions known as the frontier experience, the successive ethnically and denominationally distinct waves and strata of immigration, the rapid and nearly convulsive processes of urbanization and industrialization, the Negro problem, and the early establishment of a dominant middle-class outlook and way of life. The religious history of the country includes equally distinct circumstances: the Puritan period, the early separation of church and state, followed by a persistent and peculiarly intimate relation between politics and religion, the era of revival movements, the prodigious development of sects, and the transformation of sects into denominations.

If one views the findings of research on church religion in America against this historical background, it is surprising that they exhibit so much similarity to the European data. It is true that, at first, this similarity is not obvious. Fewer people seem to be involved in church religion than in Europe – if one bases the comparison on the European conception of nominal membership. Conversely, and no matter what criteria one uses, the figures for participation and involvement are much higher for the United States. The difference is especially striking in the case of Protestantism, since Catholic participation rates are relatively high in Europe too.

Yet, on closer inspection, it appears that the same general factors determine the over-all social location of church religion, although the levels of participation may differ. The participation rates are again higher for Catholicism than Protestantism, especially if, in the latter case, one considers the major denominations rather than some of the smaller sects. And, again, differences between rural and urban areas can be found. The contrast between city and country exhibits a more complex pattern than in Europe and is not as striking, mainly because of Catholic concentrations in many metropolitan areas. The differences between men and women also follow the same lines, with the exception of the Jews. These differences, too, are less sharply drawn than in Europe. The differences in the involvement of the generations in church religion follow the European example only in part. Here, a number of factors, especially the pull of Sunday-school children on the parents – most pronounced in suburbia – complicates the basic pattern.

From the findings on church involvement of different occupational groups, no consistent picture emerges. In any case, the data are too scarce to permit any generalizations. One may, perhaps, suspect that in this instance some deviations from the European pattern may be present. The differences between classes with respect to religion are less pronounced than in Europe. This may be attributable in part to the fact that class differences are less pronounced – and certainly less conspicuous – in general, despite an underlying structural similarity in the social stratification of the Western European countries and the United States. Although the major churches and denominations are, at the very least, middle-class oriented, the relatively sharp cleavage between a church-oriented middle class and an unchurched working class does not exist. This is, of course, not surprising, since the working class today merges almost imperceptibly into the outlook, way of life, and religious pattern of the middle classes to a much greater extent than in Europe, although there are some indications of a process of *embourgeoisement* in the European working class. Such differences as still exist in the recruitment of church members and in participation are overlaid by the peculiarly American differentiation of prestige among the denominations. These differences find expression in the composition of membership of the denominations. Significantly enough, however, the status differences in the membership of the denominations are popularly much exaggerated. In this connection the Negro-White cleavage in Protestant churches and congregations deserves to be mentioned. These observations are not valid for one social stratum: the rural and urban proletariat, the term not being understood in its Marxist sense. It consists in large part of

Negroes, Puerto Ricans, Mexicans, and others. This stratum is socially almost completely invisible and nearly unchurched. Even Catholicism, whose influence on the working class generally appears to be stronger than that of Protestantism, appears to have lost or is losing its hold on this stratum. But this stratum is not part of the middle-class oriented working population and those parts that are not unchurched tend to be attracted to sects that are marginal to Protestantism both theologically and in its orientation to society.

Ethnic churches played a significant role in American religious history. Today, ethnic churches for persons of European background have either disappeared or are of subordinate importance. Only churches linked to racial minorities persist on the religious scene. Their function depends, of course, on the position of the minorities in American society.

One of the most important developments in American church religion is the process of doctrinal leveling. It can be safely said that within Protestantism doctrinal differences are virtually irrelevant for the members of the major denominations. Even for the ministry, traditional theological differences seem to have an ever-decreasing importance. More significant is the steady leveling of the differences between Catholicism, Protestantism, and Judaism. This process should not be taken as a result of a serious theological *rapprochement*. Furthermore, several areas of fairly sharp friction remain between Catholicism and the other religious bodies, especially in matters of public policy. There can be little doubt, however, that Catholicism, Protestantism, and Judaism are jointly characterized by similar structural transformations – a bureaucratization along rational businesslike lines – and accommodation to the "secular" way of life. In consequence of the historical link between this way of life and the Protestant ethos, the accommodation of Protestantism, as represented by its major denominations, has perhaps gone farther than that of the other religious bodies. It seems, however, that the difference is superficial (cf. Herberg 1955). It is to be noted that, despite the trend toward a leveling of ideological differences and the increasing irrelevance of doctrine for the membership, the *social* differences in the traditions of Protestantism, Catholicism, and Judaism continue to play a role. According to some findings, they may be destined for perpetuation by endogamy. The way of life and the social basis for some central dimensions of subjective identification remain linked to subcultures designated by religious labels (cf. Lenski 1961).

These observations may be summarized as follows. There are some aspects of church religion in America which are either unique or at least conspicuously different from the European situation. With one exception – the relatively high involvement of Americans in church religion – the differences seem less significant than the similarities. The correlations of various indices of involvement in church religion with demographic and ecological variables as well as with social role and status configurations follow a similar pattern in the European and American findings. This pattern represents the social location of church religion in the industrial countries of the West. If we may take these countries as paradigmatic, the pattern invites the conclusion that church-oriented religion has become a marginal phenomenon in modern society.

This conclusion meets one serious difficulty in the previously mentioned deviation from the pattern. The most "modern" of the countries under discussion, the United States, shows the highest degree of involvement in church religion. To compound the difficulties, the high American figures of overt participation represent, in all likelihood, a fairly recent upward movement rather than a decrease from a yet higher previous level. In the face of these circumstances, it is obvious that no simple unilinear and one-dimensional theory of "secularization" in modern society can be maintained.

The difficulty is only apparent. In order to resolve it, it is only necessary to take into account the differences in the character of church religion in Europe and America. In Europe, church religion did not undergo radical inner transformations and became restricted to a minor part of the population. As it continued to represent and mediate the traditional universe of religious ideas, its social base shrunk characteristically to that part of the population which is peripheral to the structure of modern society: the peasantry, the remnants of the traditional bourgeoisie, and petite bourgeoisie within the middle classes, which are not – or no longer or not yet – involved in the typical work processes of industrial and urban society.[3]

In the United States, on the other hand, church religion has a broad middle-class distribution. The middle classes are, *in toto*, anything but peripheral to the modern industrial world. The distribution of church religion in America, nevertheless, does not represent a reversal of the trend toward "secularization" – that is, a resurgence of traditional church religion. It is rather the result of a radical inner change in American church religion. This change consists in the adoption of the *secular* version of the Protestant ethos by the churches which, of course, did not result from concerted policy but is rather a product of a unique constellation of factors in American social and religious history.[4]

Whereas religious ideas originally played an important part in the shaping of the American Dream, today the secular ideas of the American Dream pervade church religion. The cultural, social, and psychological functions which the churches perform for American society as a whole as well as for its social groups, classes, and individuals would be considered "secular" rather than "religious" in the view the churches traditionally held of themselves.[5] Comparing the European and American findings on the social location of church religion and allowing for the differences in the character of church religion in European and American society, we are led to the conclusion that traditional church religion was pushed to the periphery of "modern" life in Europe while it became more "modern" in America by undergoing a process of internal secularization. This conclusion requires further interpretation.

The configuration of meaning which constitutes the symbolic reality of traditional church religion appears to be unrelated to the culture of modern industrial society. It is certain, at least, that internalization of the symbolic reality of traditional religion is neither enforced nor, in the typical case, favored by the social structure of contemporary society. This fact alone suffices to explain why traditional church religion moved to the margin of contemporary life. The findings contradict the notion that the challenge of overt antichurch ideologies plays an important role. If the churches maintain their institutional claim to represent and mediate the traditional religious universe of meaning, they survive primarily by association with social groups and social strata which continue to be oriented toward the values of a past social order. If, on the other hand, the churches accommodate themselves to the dominant culture of modern industrial society, they necessarily take on the function of legitimating the latter. In the performance of this function, however, the universe of meaning traditionally represented by the churches becomes increasingly irrelevant. In short, the so-called process of secularization has decisively altered either the social location of church religion or its inner universe of meaning. As we have formulated it, it may appear that these two alternatives are mutually exclusive. This is the case only for their hypothetical, extreme forms. In fact, less radical transformations of both the social location and the meaning-universe of church religion may occur jointly.

The marginality of traditional church religion in modern society poses two distinct, although related, theoretical questions which must be answered by sociology. Since both questions refer to the problem of secularization as the term is commonly understood, it will be useful to state the questions separately. First, it is necessary to identify the causes which pushed traditional church religion to the periphery of modern society and to give an account of the latter process in terms consistent with general sociological theory. Second, it is necessary to ask whether anything that could be called religion in the framework of sociological analysis replaced traditional church religion in modern society.

It is obvious that, until the present, the sociology of religion was only concerned with the first question. We said before that the sociology of religion found itself in a serious theoretical predicament when trying to give an account of secularization. Starting from the premise that church and religion were essentially one, its own findings led the discipline to the conclusion that religion, the term understood in its most general sense, becomes a marginal phenomenon in modern society – unless it ceases to be religion. The logic of the argument demanded that global causes be found for such a transformation. Since we need not accept the premise, we can avoid that predicament. We need not look for global causes to account for the fate that befell the universe of meaning based upon a particular, historical, social institution. Whereas the problem is theoretically more restricted than commonly thought, it is, of course, still more relevant than, for example, a process of change from the extended to the nuclear family – at least if that process is viewed in isolation. Furthermore, this question is – as we just indicated – linked to the second, more important problem to be discussed. A few observations are, therefore, in order here.

In identifying the causes of secularization, it does not suffice to refer to industrialization and urbanization as though these processes would automatically and necessarily undermine the values of traditional church religion. On the other hand, one cannot adequately interpret the decrease in church religion as a retreat before a historical wave of hostile ideologies and value systems such as various types of "faith" in science. To postulate that the latter possess some inherent superiority – if only of a pragmatic kind – is sociologically downright naïve. It is more consistent with general sociological theory to view industrialization and urbanization as specific socio-historical processes which, however, led to encompassing changes in the total social structure. Once the nature of these changes is better understood, it will be possible to specify more adequately the concomitant transformation in the pattern of individual life in society – and the decreasing role of traditional church religion in lending meaning to that pattern. It is often overlooked that the relation between industrialization and secularization is indirect. The corresponding explanatory schemes are, therefore, either too narrowly structural, deriving the change in one institution from changes in another, presumably more "basic" institution, or remain restricted to the history of ideas, interpreting the process as the replacement of one system of values by another, presumably more "powerful" one.

In suggesting that the relation between industrialization and secularization is indirect, we gain a different perspective on the process. The values which were originally institutionalized by church religion were not the norms of a particular action system. To put it differently, the values originally underlying church religion were not institutional norms but norms lending significance to individual life in its totality. As such they were superordinated to the norms of all the institutions that determined the conduct of individuals in various spheres of everyday life and spanned their biographies. Industrialization and urbanization were processes that reinforced the tendency of institutional specialization. Institutional specialization, in turn, tended to "free" the norms of the various institutional areas from the influence of the originally superordinated "religious" values. As we shall try to show later, the significance of these values for the individual decreased as they became irrelevant in his economic, political, and other activities. In other words, the reality of the religious cosmos waned in proportion to its shrinking social base; to wit, specialized religious institutions. What were originally total life values became part-time norms. In short, the decrease in traditional church religion may be seen as a consequence of the shrinking relevance of the values, institutionalized in church religion, for the integration and legitimation of everyday life in modern society.

If the answer we suggested to the first question referring to the problem of secularization is correct, one task for the sociology of religion consists in explaining the limited and modified persistence of church religion in the contemporary world. This task may be considered as solved, at least in part. The findings of the recent sociology of religion indicate, as we pointed out before, that traditional church religion came to depend more and more upon social groups and strata that are, in a sense, survivals of a past social order within modern society (cf. Tenbruck 1959).

The shrinking of church religion, however, is only one – and the sociologically less interesting – dimension of the problem of secularization. For the analysis of contemporary society another question is more important. What are the dominant values overarching contemporary culture? What is the social-structural basis of these values and what is their function in the life of contemporary man? For the sociologist, it is not enough to trivialize the view that secularization refers to the retreat of religion before the onslaught of materialism, modern paganism, and the like. He must ask, rather, what it is that secularization has brought about in the way of a socially objectivated cosmos of meaning. The survival of traditional forms of church religion, the absence, in the West, of an institutionalized antichurch, and the overwhelming significance of Christianity in the shaping of the modern Western world have combined in obscuring the possibility that a new religion is in the making. It is this possibility that we shall try to raise from a purely speculative status to the status of a productive hypothesis in the sociological theory of religion.

Notes

1 Notable are Fichter's studies of Catholic parishes. Fichter was influential in initiating the trend from purely sociographic studies to parish sociology and his studies served as a model for most recent Catholic as well as Protestant parish investigations (cf. Fichter 1951, 1954).

2 Considering the limitations of this study an attempt to document the following by a complete bibliography would be impossible. A large bibliography can be found in Goldschmidt & Matthes 1962; For reviews of the field see Glock 1959: 153–177; Honigsheim 1957: 450–481; Hunt 1958; Le Bras 1960: 79–102; Goldschmidt et al. 1959; Lambert 1960.

3 For an interpretation see Tenbruck 1959; cf. also Koester 1959, esp. p. 108.

4 A study which traces the symptoms of these changes has been done by Schneider & Dornbusch 1958.

5 For a description and interpretation of these functions see Berger 1961.

III

THE ANTHROPOLOGICAL CONDITION OF RELIGION

It is easy to understand why religion is commonly identified with one of its particular forms; that is, the form in which it appears in the history of Western society. It was in this form that religion became an impressive and yet familiar reality for many generations. What is more important, it was essentially in this form that religion became the subject of much theological and philosophical reflection. Yet, if we accept this identification, the findings of the recent sociology of religion would have us believe that religion is an exceptional phenomenon in society. This, indeed, is a view that is compatible with Christian, and especially Protestant, theology. The distinction between "natural" religions and Christianity assigns the former to "the world" while insisting on the exceptional character of Christian faith. For theological reasons, the latter finds itself antithetical to society. This position is, of course, most sharply articulated in Neo-orthodox theology. If we disregard, for a moment, the context in which the view is formulated, we find, interestingly enough, that various dialectical and positivist philosophies of history arrive at an analogous position. Taking account of historical and ethnological data, these would accord a broader social basis to religion in earlier periods and to societies that find themselves in an earlier stage of "social evolution" but would not doubt its exceptional character in modern society. Different as they are in other respects, these positions share the conviction that the emerging modern world is characterized by the absence of religion or a regression to "natural" religion.

Under the impression of a particular historical form of religion, a misleadingly general definition of religion emerged. This definition is substantive rather than functional. It should be obvious that it is the substantive character of the definition which explains the surprising similarities in positions otherwise so

DOI: 10.4324/9781003257875-4

divergent. True, the substantive character of the definition invites evaluations and the evaluations differ sharply. Yet it matters little whether religion, thus defined, is evaluated positively or negatively, explicitly or implicitly. The definition prejudges the phenomenon in a manner which is best described as narrowly "ethnocentric." Whatever the theological and philosophical merits of these views, they are based on a definition of religion that is of no value to sociology.

By way of comparison, we may note that, at present, nobody would seriously doubt that economic or political phenomena are universal elements of social life; to be found, in forms to be discovered and analyzed, even in societies in which economic or political phenomena, comparable, say, to a market economy or the nation-state, are lacking – to be found, in fact, in societies in which fully developed economic and political institutions do not exist. But then, economic and political phenomena are defined, in sociology, by functional rather than substantive criteria. Some of the difficulties in the sociological theory of religion are due to the fact that this is not generally the case for religion. Once a substantive definition of religion has been accepted one can, of course, hopefully or fearfully raise the question whether religion is, or has become, an exceptional phenonmenon. If we take up the suggestion submitted by Durkheim – or, at least, implied in his work – and define religion by its universal social function that question ceases to make sense. In order to be useful for the sociological theory of religion, the suggestion must be specified. This will involve some difficulties which we shall try to overcome. One thing, however, can be asserted confidently here. A functional definition of religion avoids both the customary ideological bias and the "ethnocentric" narrowness of the substantive definition of the phenomenon.

The term "function" is used in varied meanings in the several sciences dealing with man. We must, therefore, begin by specifying the sense it has in the present discussion. It need hardly be stressed that we do not propose to follow the explanatory procedures of psychological functionalism. Little would be gained by discovering that religion performs some intrapsychic functions, unless we could first account for the constitution, as a social fact, of that which is capable of performing such functions for the individual. To derive religion from some alleged intrapsychic mechanism of a hypothetical *homo psychologicus* would be manifestly absurd. The conceptual framework of sociological functionalism also fails in providing an answer to our basic question. We may be inclined, perhaps, to turn to it for explanatory schemes in the study of societies which possess specialized religious institutions. One should not preclude, a priori, the possibility that a structural-functional analysis, for example, might illuminate the relation between economic, political, and religious institutions in some societies. Unfortunately, however, sociological functionalism, as exemplified today by structural-functionalism, presupposes precisely what is put in question here. Religious institutions are not universal; the phenomena underlying religious institutions or, to put it differently, performing analogous functions in the relation of the individual and the social order presumably are universal. We must, therefore, consider problematic what is taken for granted in sociological functionalism. What are the general anthropological conditions for that which may become institutionalized as religion? What reality does it possess, as a social fact, even before it is institutionalized? How is it constituted before it assumes one of the variable historical forms of religious institutions? Is it possible to specify the conditions under which it does become an institution?

These are questions of considerable generality. And yet, as can be readily seen, they should be considered in relation to still more general theoretical problems. The familiar forms of religion known to us as tribal religion, ancestor cult, church, sect, and so forth are specific historical institutionalizations of symbolic universes. Symbolic universes are socially objectivated systems of meaning that refer, on the one hand, to the world of everyday life and point, on the other hand, to a world that is experienced as transcending everyday life.[6] In order to answer our initial questions, we must, therefore, ascertain how symbolic universes in general, and a religious cosmos in particular, are socially objectivated. As the next step, we must investigate the conditions under which the social basis of a religious cosmos is institutionalized. Such considerations, however, clearly lead to general problems of institutional theory and the sociology of knowledge and, ultimately, conduct us beyond the scope of sociological theory proper into the field of philosophical anthropology. How are subjective processes objectivated in society? How are socially objectivated phenomena institutionalized and what are the functions of institutionalization? How do institutionalization and objectivation, once they have produced social realities, affect the subjective processes in which institutionalization and objectivation are rooted?

It must be immediately admitted that it will be impossible to analyze adequately these general problems in the present essay. The argument by which we shall try to develop answers to our initial questions demands, however, that certain aspects of these general problems, at least, be clarified. We shall try to do so as fully as the present context will allow.[7]

As we just said, symbolic universes are objectivated meaning-systems that relate the experiences of everyday life to a "transcendent" layer of reality. Other systems of meaning do not point beyond the world of everyday life; that is, they do not contain a "transcendent" reference. The peculiar significance of symbolic universes will have to be discussed in more detail later on. Now we must consider a quality that is common to all meaning-systems: they are constructed of objectivations.

Objectivations are the products of subjective activities that become available as elements in a common world both to their producers and to other men (cf. Berger & Luckmann 1966: 33 ff.). While expressions are available only in face-to-face situations, objectivations serve as indices of meaning outside such limitations of space and time. Objectivations are essentially social. Since the construction of symbolic universes as systems of meaning occurs by means of objectivations, it is evident that we cannot consider them as a summation of isolated subjective processes. Furthermore, the maintenance of symbolic universes over the generations – and hence their establishment as a key element of social tradition – rests on processes of social transmission. But the statement that symbolic universes are social in origin is valid in an additional and more elementary sense. The objectivation of a symbolic universe as a system of meaning presupposes that the subjective experiences entering into its construction be meaningful. The meaningful quality of subjective experience, however, is a product of social processes.

Subjective experience considered in isolation is restricted to mere actuality and is void of meaning. Meaning is not an inherent quality of subjective processes but is bestowed on it in interpretive acts. In such acts, a subjective process is grasped retrospectively and located in an interpretive scheme. Such "meaning" as may be superimposed on ongoing experiences is necessarily derived from prior – eventually habitualized – interpretive acts. In other words, the meaning of experience depends, strictly speaking, upon one's "stopping and thinking"; that is, acts by which subjective processes are located in an interpretive scheme. The interpretive scheme is necessarily distinct from ongoing experience. If we may use the term in its most elementary sense, we may say that the interpretive scheme "transcends" ongoing experience.

Interpretive schemes result from sediment past experiences. The relation between experience, its meaning and interpretive scheme is reciprocal and dynamic. The meaning of experience is derived from the relation of ongoing processes to the scheme of interpretation. Conversely, ongoing experiences modify the interpretive scheme. The very possibility of successive experience being sedimented in a scheme distinct from any actual experience rests upon a certain degree of detachment. Such detachment cannot originate in a simple succession of isolated subjective processes. Now it is true that a genuinely isolated subjective process is inconceivable. At the very least, each ongoing experience has a temporal horizon of past and anticipated experiences.[8]

The phaselike character of subjective processes may provide the basis for an elementary scheme of interpretation by which ongoing, past, and anticipated experiences are set in relation to each other in conscious acts. As the phrase "to stop and think" indicates, such acts presuppose that the individual can detach himself from the actuality and immediacy of ongoing experiences while turning to past or anticipating future experiences. Such detachment is nothing that a human organism could reach by itself. Organisms are placed in an environment with a given instinctual equipment. The behavior of an organism is determined by the interplay of environment, instinct, and an element of learning. These are, however, notoriously inadequate in explaining human conduct – unless the biological concept of environment is unduly extended to include "society" and "culture" and the concept of instinct extended to include vague notions such as "drives" and "needs." A human organism considered in a rigorously biological perspective would be wrapped up, as it were, in the immediacy of its ongoing experiences. It could learn from past experience, but experience could not be sedimented into interpretive schemes. In other words, a human organism could not detach itself, on its own, from ongoing experience and interpret it in the light of past experience. Nor could it plan future conduct, choosing among alternatives, since this, too, would presuppose detachment from the "specious present." In spite of possessing a body with an "interior" distinct from its environment and being capable of learning to a higher degree than other animals, a human organism, thrown back upon its biological resources, would lack the temporal dimensions in which ongoing experience could become meaningful. It would not have a distinct and memorable past nor an "open" future with alternative choices of action. Its life could not develop a coherent shape as a biography. In sum, a human organism could not create meaning autonomously. To put it differently, it could not develop into an individual Self.

The direction of these observations should show that we are not concerned here with the phylogenetic question of how "culture" originally emerged. The answer would have to take into account a wide range of biological and physiological conditions; for example, the evolution of the hand and upright posture, specific developments such as the "invention" of tools, as well as a reconstruction of the concrete forms of social life in early mankind (cf. Washburn 1962). In the present context, we want to emphasize that the individuation of consciousness is a possibility of the human organism which is realized only in social processes. Returning to the main line of our argument we may say that social processes are the basis for the detachment that is presupposed in the construction of interpretive schemes "transcending" the flux of immediate experience. Now we shall have to show why this is so.[9]

Detachment from the flux of one's own experiences results from participation in the experiences of a fellow man. This becomes possible in the face-to-face situation in which the subjective processes of one partner find expression in events in shared space and time and thus become observable to the other partner. In the shared situation, the subjective processes of both are synchronized phase by phase.[10] It is of special importance for our considerations that participation in the subjective processes of the fellow man is mediated through events in space and time. The participation involves interpretation of these events and is, of course, accompanied by a certain degree of detachment. A measure of detachment thus characterizes, originally, the mediated experience of another man and is not given in the flux of one's own immediate experiences. Furthermore, the events by which another man's subjective processes are mediated are more "objective" than one's own "inner" experiences. Now in the face-to-face situation, the experiences one has of the partner are attuned to one's own ongoing "inner" experiences – but in a certain detachment from them. In other words, they are interpretations of these experiences from an independent perspective. In the synchronized flux of shared experience these interpretations, in turn, manifest themselves and become available to the first partner. Thereby an independent and quasi-objective perspective on his own experiences also becomes available to him. To sum up, while detachment from the flux of immediate experience cannot arise autonomously, it can be "imported" in the form of an "external" point of view. One begins to look at oneself through the eyes of a fellow man. This is originally possible only in the reciprocal social processes of a face-to-face situation.[11]

Detachment is the presupposition for the construction of the most elementary framework of interpretation relating past, present, and future experiences. Within this framework, a multitude of specific and differentiated interpretive schemes can be housed. Once a certain level of the individuation of consciousness and a corresponding command of language are reached, ready-made – that is, socially prefabricated – interpretive schemes can be imported *en bloc*. Conversely, detachment, originally impossible for the isolated individual, becomes a crucial dimension of personal identity and can be exercised outside of and independently from social processes. Consequently, the individual now *can* create meaning.

Another important dimension of personal identity is the integration of the subjective processes of recollection and projection into the future into the moral unity of a biography. Like the detachment from the flux of immediate experience, such integration, too, is of social origin. While detachment can be traced to the structure of face-to-face situations, such integration is to be attributed to the continuity of social relations in the life of an individual. In the succession of face-to-face situations and other less direct relations involving fellow men, the individual meets witnesses of his past, as well as potential witnesses of his future conduct. He is and will be reminded of his past. Indeed, he can be taken to task for actions he may have forgotten already.[12]

Also, he must anticipate being taken to task again for his present conduct. Subjective processes of recollection and anticipation are woven into a pattern of memory which contains the recollections and anticipations of other individuals. As they become part of such a pattern, the subjective processes become stabilized; they partake of an "objective" reality. Individual conduct is not only recalled but judged by others; it becomes a sequence of distinct and irrevocable actions. Individual conduct becomes part of an "objective" as well as moral reality. In other words, subjective experience and individual actions are integrated, in the course of continuous social relations, into a determinate and more or less coherent biography for which the individual is held accountable.

These considerations may be summed up as follows. Detachment from immediate experience originates in the confrontation with fellow men in the face-to-face situation. It leads to the individuation of consciousness and permits the construction of interpretive schemes, ultimately, of systems of meaning. Detachment from immediate experience finds its complement in the integration of past, present, and future into a socially defined, morally relevant biography. This integration develops in continuous social relations and leads to the formation of conscience. The individuation of the two complementary aspects of Self occurs in social processes. The organism – in isolation nothing but a separate pole of "meaningless" subjective processes – becomes a Self by embarking with others upon the construction of an "objective" and moral universe of meaning. Thereby the organism transcends its biological nature.

It is in keeping with an elementary sense of the concept of religion to call the transcendence of biological nature by the human organism a religious phenomenon. As we have tried to show, this phenomenon rests upon the functional relation of Self and society. We may, therefore, regard the social processes that lead to the formation of Self as fundamentally religious. This view, incidentally, does no violence to the etymology of the term. It may be objected from a theological and "substantivist" position on religion that in this view religion becomes an all-encompassing phenomenon. We suggest that this is not a valid objection. The transcendence of biological nature *is* a universal phenomenon of mankind. Another objection is to be taken more seriously. It may be said that calling the processes that lead to the formation of Self religious does, perhaps, avoid a sociologistic identification of society and religion but also fails to provide a specific account of the "objective" and institutional forms of religion in society. We plead guilty to this charge. The analysis so far did no more than identify the general source from which spring the historically differentiated social forms of religion. We would contend, however, that this represents a necessary first step in the sociological theory of religion. In showing the religious quality of the social processes by which consciousness and conscience are individuated, we identified the universal yet specific anthropological condition of religion.

Notes

6 For an analysis of different universes of meaning and their relation to the paramount reality of everyday life see Schutz 1962, esp. Part III: "On Multiple Realities," pp. 207–259 and "Symbol, Reality and Society," pp. 287–356.

7 For a systematic investigation of these problems see Berger & Luckmann 1966.

8 We may refer here to Bergson's analysis of *duree,* William James' concept of the stream of consciousness and Husserl's analysis of temporality.

9 The following analysis is based on the social psychology of George H. Mead (cf., esp. Mead 1934) and Charles H. Cooley's theory of socialization (cf. Cooley 1922, and Cooley 1909).

10 For a highly important formal analysis of the face-to-face situation see Schutz 1964, esp. pp. 23–33.

11 Cf. Sartre's highly interesting analysis of the constitution of identity which, however, fails to realize fully the importance of social processes. Sartre 1957, esp. the passages explicating Rimbaud's sentence, "I is *an other,*" on p. 97 and 98.

12 On the social dimensions of memory and time cf. Halbwachs 1925, and Halbwachs 1950.

IV
THE SOCIAL FORMS OF RELIGION

In the sociological theory of religion, it is customary to define certain ideas – for example, those dealing with the "supernatural" – as religious and, then, to attach that label to the groups and institutions that seem primarily concerned with the codification, maintenance, and propagation of such ideas. This appeared to us as a theoretically impermissible short cut. In order to avoid it, we felt obliged to begin with a specification of the universal anthropological condition of religion before turning to the question of how religion becomes a distinct part of social reality; that is, how it is objectivated socially. With this aim in mind, we gave a brief account of the origin of meaning-systems, in general, and symbolic universes, in particular, in social processes. We found that the construction of meaning-systems rested on detachment and integration and that these phenomena presupposed the reciprocity of face-to-face situations and the continuity of social relations, respectively. The formal description of the structure of social processes in which meaning-systems originated also specified the conditions for the individuation of consciousness and conscience. The formal argument led us to the similarly formal conclusion that an organism becomes a Self by constructing, with others, an "objective and moral universe of meaning." We said that the organism transcends its biological nature by developing a Self and felt justified in calling that process fundamentally religious.

Presently, we must reconsider the validity of this conclusion. Because we first had to account for the conditions under which meaning-systems could emerge, we had to restrict our analysis to the constitutive elements of the social processes in which consciousness and conscience are individuated and meaning-systems constructed. We had to leave out of our consideration the historical priority of meaning-systems to any particular human organism.

DOI: 10.4324/9781003257875-5

The conclusion to which our formal analysis led us is, therefore, valid only on the level of general anthropological discourse. We had to restrict our analysis to this level, temporarily, for an obvious reason. The historical existence of meaning-systems is the result of universe-constructing activities of successive generations (cf. Berger & Luckmann 1966: esp. 85–118). Had we started out with the proposition that universes of meaning are historically given, we could not have avoided an infinite regression in our analysis. We did avoid it by giving, first, a formal description of the general conditions under which universes of meaning are constructed. Now we have reached the point, however, at which we may abandon our initial and selfimposed restriction and give due attention to an empirical fact that we so far disregarded.

Empirically, human organisms do not construct "objective" and moral universes of meaning from scratch – they are born into them. This means that human organisms normally transcend their biological nature by internalizing a historically given universe of meaning, rather than by constructing universes of meaning. This implies, further, that a human organism does not confront other human organisms; it confronts Selves. While we so far described the formal structure only of the social processes in which a Self emerges, we must now add that these processes are always filled with "content." To put it differently, the human organism becomes a Self in concrete processes of socialization. These processes exhibit the formal structure previously described *and* mediate, empirically, a historical social order. We suggested before that the transcendence of biological nature by human organisms is a fundamentally religious process. We may now continue by saying that socialization, as the concrete process in which such transcendence is achieved, is fundamentally religious. It rests on the universal anthropological condition of religion, individuation of consciousness, and conscience in social processes, and is actualized in the internalization of the configuration of meaning underlying a historical social order. We shall call this configuration of meaning a world view.

The world view transcends the individual in several ways. It is a historical reality which precedes the individuation of any organism's consciousness and conscience. Once it is internalized, it becomes a subjective reality for the individual and circumscribes for him the range of meaningful and potentially meaningful experience. Thus it determines his orientation in the world and exerts an influence upon his conduct that is as profound as it is taken for granted and, therefore, unnoticed. In addition, the world view exerts an indirect and "external" influence upon the conduct of the individual by means of institutionalized and noninstitutionalized social controls, which reflect the social order and its underlying configuration of meaning. The world view is, consequently, an objective and historical (transcendent), as well as a subjective (immanent), reality for the individual.

Under certain circumstances, the world view may reach a further level of transcendence. Since the social order is apprehended as valid and obligatory regardless of person, place, and situation, it can be understood as a manifestation of a transcendent and universal order, as a *cosmion* reflecting a cosmos (cf. Voegelin 1952: esp. 27). It may be added that the procedure by which a world view is assigned the status of universality and the transcendence of the social order is explicitly articulated typically serves as a mechanism of great significance in the legitimation of an established social order (cf. Berger & Luckmann 1966: esp. 85–96).

The very fact that the world view is a socially objectivated historical reality explains its crucial function for the individual. Instead of constructing a rudimentary system of meaning, the individual draws upon a reservoir of significance. The world view, as the result of universe-constructing activities of successive generations, is immeasurably richer and more differentiated than the interpretive schemes that could be developed from scratch by individuals. Its stability, as a socially objectivated reality, is immeasurably greater than that of individual streams of consciousness. The world view, as a transcendent moral universe, has an obligatory character that could not be approximated in the immediate context of social relations.

Individual existence derives its meaning from a transcendent world view. The stability of the latter makes it possible for the individual to grasp a sequence of originally disjointed situations as a significant biographical whole. The world view as a historical matrix of meaning spans the life of the individual and the life of generations. We may say, in sum, that the historical priority of a world view provides the empirical basis for the "successful" transcendence of biological nature by human organisms, detaching the latter from their immediate life context and integrating them, as persons, into the context of a tradition of meaning. We may conclude, therefore, that the world view, as an "objective" and historical social reality, performs an essentially religious function and define it as an *elementary social form of religion*. This social form is universal in human society.

The world view is an encompassing system of meaning in which socially relevant categories of time, space, causality, and purpose are superordinated to more specific interpretive schemes in which reality is segmented and the segments related to one another. In other words, it contains a "natural" logic as well as a "natural" taxonomy. It is important to note that both the logic and the taxonomy have a pragmatic as well as a moral dimension. We say that the logic and the taxonomy contained in a world view are "natural" because they are taken for granted in their totality without question. Only particular items, especially in the content of taxonomic areas, can become doubtful within the lifetime of an individual. As long as the social structure and the social order remain in existence, the logic, at least, survives the passing of many generations. In stable societies, however, not only the logic but also the taxonomy gives the appearance of permanence and rigidity.

In connection with these observations, it should be stressed that socialization consists in the internalization of the world view as an encompassing configuration of meaning. The learning of particular items of content is, of course, part of the process and the part which can be apprehended as a conscious performance. In contrast, the internalization of the encompassing configuration of meaning, while containing the acquisition of particular items of content, is not conscious in the same sense. It can be observed only as the formation of an individual "style" of thinking and acting that is relatively independent of the particular characteristics of a given situation and that can be attributed only to the "character" of a person.

The world view is objectivated in society in various forms. Some socially approved and significant ways of orientation in nature and society manifest themselves in stylized forms of movement, gesture, and expression that are transmitted from generation to generation. Some socially significant moral ideas and values are represented by symbols of various kinds; for example, flags, icons, totems. The most important form in which a world view is socially objectivated, however, is language. Before showing why this is the case a remark on the relation of world view and language is in order.

At first, one might be tempted to consider the social structure in its totality as an objectivation of the world view. The social structure as a system of performances is, indeed, oriented by the world view. But performances are acts of individuals and one should not disregard the fact that they are directly based upon a substratum of "meaningless" physiological processes, biological needs, and so forth. On the other hand, performances are determined directly or indirectly by institutional controls. Despite the fact that institutional controls reflect in some fashion the configuration of meaning underlying the world view, the fact cannot be ignored that norms can be and are enforced regardless of what is subjectively meaningful to an individual. It would be, therefore, imprecise as well as confusing to consider the social structure as a "straightforward" objectivation of the world view. The world view stands in a dialectic relationship with the social structure. It originates in human activities that are at least partly institutionalized. It is transmitted over the generations in processes that are, again, at least partly dependent on institutions. Conversely, performances and institutions depend on the continuous internalization of a world view.

We said that the most important objectivation of the world view is to be found in language. A language contains the most comprehensive and, at the same time, most highly differentiated system of interpretation. This system can be internalized, in principle, by any member of society, and all experiences of all members can be potentially located in that system. The logic and the taxonomy contained in the world view are stabilized in the syntax and the semantic structure of the language. It is obvious, therefore, that in the analysis of the objectivating function of language its semantic and syntactic levels are of more immediate consequence than its phonology. It is just as obvious, however, that it is the embodiment of sense in sound which fixes and stabilizes interpretive schemes and makes the latter continuously and routinely available.

We said earlier that socialization consists, concretely, in the learning of particular items of content but that these are only elements in the internalizations of an encompassing configuration of meaning. Analogously, the learning of particular linguistic elements, while essential and the only directly observable and conscious process, is subordinate to the internalization of what we may call, adopting Wilhelm von Humboldt's concept, the inner form of language.[13]

The explicit rules and codifications, corresponding roughly to what in linguistics are called "phenotypes," are, of course, objectivations in the strict sense. At least as important, however, are the contextual elements in the linguistic analysis of reality, the "cryptotypes." The explicit and the contextual elements together constitute the inner form of language – the latter may be said to represent a comprehensive model of the universe.[14]

As the individual acquires his mother tongue and internalizes its inner form, he takes over the "natural" logic and taxonomy of a historical world view. The world view, as a reservoir of ready-made solutions and as a matrix of procedures for solving problems, routinizes and stabilizes the individual's memory, thinking, conduct, and perception in a manner that is inconceivable without the mediation of language. Through language, the world view serves the individual as a source of meaning that is continuously available – both internally and socially.

We defined the world view as an elementary social form of religion. This definition rests on two assumptions which we tried to establish in the foregoing analysis: that the world view performs an essentially religious function and that it is part of socially objectivated reality. One difficulty, however, that may be read into this definition still needs to be clarified.

The world view, as an encompassing system of meaning, contains typifications, interpretive schemes, and recipes for conduct on different levels of generality. Those on the lower levels refer to routine affairs and matters of everyday life (such as, the west wind brings rain; don't eat raw pork). Taken by themselves, they appear too trivial to deserve to be designated as "religious." But our analysis – at least up to the present point – does not imply that any single element of the world view, trivial or otherwise, is "religious." No single interpretive scheme performs a religious function. It is, rather, the world view as a whole, as a unitary matrix of meaning, that provides the historical context within which human organisms form identities, thereby transcending biological nature.

It will be, therefore, advisable to add an explicit reminder of this fact to the definition of the world view as a social form of religion and say that it is both elementary and *nonspecific*. Perhaps, it is superfluous to point out that the nonspecific quality of the world view – as a social form of religion – is connected with another previously mentioned circumstance. The world view is universal in human society and has no special or distinct institutional basis. It stands, rather, in a dialectic relationship to the social structure as a whole. Important as it was to establish the religious function and the social "objectivity" of the world view, the sociological theory of religion, interested in specific forms of religion in society, cannot rest content at that point. We must, therefore, now turn to the question of what additional and distinctly articulated forms religion may assume in society and how such forms are to be derived from the elementary and nonspecific objectivation of religion in the world view.

Although we just said that the world view as a whole performs a religious function and that no single element of the world view is to be designated as religious, we must presently qualify this statement. Within the world view, a domain of meaning can become articulated that deserves to be called religious. This domain consists of symbols which represent an essential "structural" trait of the world view as a whole – to wit, its inner hierarchy of significance. It is the fact that this domain stands for the religious function of the world view as a whole that justifies calling it religious.

The typifications, interpretive schemes, and models of conduct contained in a world view are not discrete and isolated units of meaning. They are arranged in a hierarchy of significance. Formally speaking, this hierarchical arrangement of meaning is an essential "structural" trait of the world view. The concrete arrangement of the elements in a historical world view, however, is a characteristic that distinguishes it empirically from other historical world views. The extraordinary richness of the permutations of meaning and the historical variety of the hierarchies of significance preclude a detailed analysis. We shall have to restrict ourselves to a formal outline of the argument, illustrating, rather than systematically documenting the argument, by occasional examples.

On the lowest level of the world view are typifications of concrete objects and events in the world of everyday life (trees, rocks, dogs, walking, running, eating, green, round, etc.). These typifications are applied routinely and in an attitude of familiarity in the course of unproblematic experiences. While they aid in the articulation of such experiences, they instill little significance into them. The interpretive schemes and recipes for conduct on the next higher level are based on the typifications of the first level, but contain, in addition, significant elements of pragmatic *and* "moral" evaluation (such as, maize does not grow where aloe grows; pork is inferior meat; there should be no marriage between first-degree cousins; if invited for dinner, take flowers to the lady of the house). Such schemes and recipes are also applied in taken-for-granted processes of orientation in everyday life, but are charged with some significance that points "beyond" the individual experience and are capable of functioning as "motives." To this level are superordinated more general interpretive schemes and models of conduct which chart a morally significant course of thought and conduct against a background of problematic alternatives (such as, early to bed and early to rise keeps a man healthy, wealthy, and wise; a true warrior does not shrink from pain; and a lady does not smoke in public). The application of these models and interpretive schemes in concrete instances depends on an element of reflection – as slight as that may be – and is, typically, accompanied by a subjective realization of the "moral" significance involved. These models and schemes are closely linked to evaluations and prescriptions formulated in terms of encompassing biographical categories (such as, he lived and died a man). These are related, in turn, to a superordinated level of interpretation referring to social and historical wholes (such as, a just social order; the beaver clan) that claim jurisdiction over individual conduct.

Thus, as one moves from the lower to the higher levels of meaning in a world view, one finds a decrease of familiar and variable concreteness that is met with unthinking routine and an increase of generally obligatory models whose concrete application involves some "choice." This complex hierarchy of significance is a "structural" trait of the world view. As we indicated earlier, it is capable of articulation. Such articulation is necessarily indirect: The hierarchy of significance underlying world view as a whole finds expression in *specific* representations. These representations implicitly stand for the global sense of the world view but refer, explicitly, to a distinct level of reality – a level in which ultimate significance is located. Thus a "structural" trait of the world view becomes a part of its "contents."

The routines of everyday life "make sense" in graduated biographical, social, and historical strata of meaning. Daily life is apprehended as being subordinated to levels of significance that transcend everyday life. Everyday routines are part and parcel of a familiar world. This is a world which can be managed by ordinary action. Its "reality" can be grasped by the ordinary senses of ordinary men. The "reality" of the world of everyday life is concrete, unproblematic and, as we may say, "profane." The strata of significance to which everyday life is ultimately referred, however, are neither concrete nor unproblematic. Their "reality" manifests itself in various ways which are only partially accessible to the insight of ordinary men. That "reality" cannot be dealt with habitually; indeed, it is beyond the control of ordinary men. The domain transcending the world of everyday life is experienced as "different" and mysterious. If the characteristic quality of everyday life is its "profaneness," the quality that defines the transcendent domain is its "sacredness."

The relation between the world of everyday life and the sacred domain is indirect. Many graduated strata of meaning mediate between the trivial and "profane" routines and the "ultimate" significance of a biography, a social tradition, and so forth. There is another type of experience which results from a breakdown of the routine of everyday life. It ranges from helplessness in the face of natural events to death and is typically accompanied by anxiety or ecstasy or a mixture of both. Experiences of that type are apprehended, as a rule, as direct manifestations of the reality of the sacred domain. Thus both the ultimate significance of everyday life and the meaning of extraordinary experiences are located in this "different" and "sacred" domain of reality.

While the two domains tend to become polarized, they are necessarily apprehended as being related in some manner. This relationship ranges from a relatively high degree of segregation between a profane world and a sacred cosmos to a high degree of interpenetration. Animism, totemism, and eschatology are some of the more typical systematic elaborations of this relationship.

Since the sacred cosmos is taken to manifest itself in the profane world in some form, there is no insurmountable obstacle to an articulation of the transcendent domain in the world of everyday life. The articulation depends, however, on the "limited" objective possibilities of expression that characterize the profane world. Consequently, there is a tendency to consider such expression as "ultimately" inadequate. Again one finds a variety of more or less systematic positions on this question, ranging from the view that the sacred cosmos manifests itself in concrete and visible enclaves in the profane world to highly sophisticated theories of the roles which language, icons, and so forth perform in expressing the "inexpressible."

We must now qualify the statement that the articulation of the sacred cosmos depends on the possibilities of ordinary expression. It is valid in a purely formal sense: The sacred cosmos is, of course, socially objectivated in the same media in which the world view as a whole is objectivated – that is, in performances, images, and language. Formally speaking, rituals are performances, sacred icons are images, divine names are words. Yet there is a difference. Performances such as a manner of eating and a procedure of planting do indeed embody an aspect of the world view. The meaning of such performances is, however, first and foremost, pragmatic. They have a purpose in the context of everyday life proper, but only indirectly are they integrated into "higher" levels of significance. Ritual acts, on the other hand, which embody an element of the sacred cosmos, are – strictly speaking – meaningless within the immediate context of everyday life. Their purpose refers *directly* to the sacred cosmos. Sacrifices, rites of passage, burial rites, and such like represent ultimate significance without what we may term intermediate levels of translation into the profane context of everyday routine. *Mutatis mutandis*, this also holds for language, the most important medium of objectivation of the world view in general as well as of the sacred cosmos. The formulation of interpretive schemes and models of conduct in everyday life depends, primarily, upon the straightforward referential function of language. The linguistic articulation of a sacred cosmos, however, rests upon what we may term the symbolic potential of language which appears in the personification of events, the formation of divine names, the construction of "different" realities by metaphorical transposition, and so forth (Cf. for example Snell 1955: esp. 17–42; Webster 1952–53: 1–22). In contrast to ordinary use, the symbolic use of language is typically accompanied by an element of ecstasy and frequently leads to a theory of inspiration.

In sum, language combines with ritual acts and icons in the articulation of a sacred cosmos. The most prominent objectivated features of this cosmos are a sacred calendar, a sacred topography, and ritual enactments of the sacred tradition of social groups, as well as ritual acts instilling sacred significance into individual biographies. Further elaborations of the sacred cosmos may take the form of thematically rather specific condensation of critical problems of social and individual life in dance, epos, drama.

The embodiments of the sacred cosmos – which we shall call religious representations – authoritatively bestow sense to individual life. The authority of religious representations cannot be derived from the content of a given sacred theme taken in isolation. It rests upon the hierarchy of significance of the world view as a whole and, ultimately, upon the transcendent quality of the latter. The integrating function of the world view as a whole is performed in concrete processes of socialization by specific religious representations. The effectiveness of specific religious themes in shaping individual consciousness and in bestowing significance upon individual biographies, however, does not originate in the explicit, historically variable content of the themes but in the hierarchy of significance which these themes indirectly represent. The explicitly articulated transcendence of a sacred cosmos in relation to the world of everyday life stands for the transcendence of a socially articulated world view in relation to the subjective stream of consciousness. Correspondingly, the specifically articulated religious themes in the process of socialization stand for socialization as a total process of religious individuation.

We may say, in summary, that the hierarchy of significance which characterizes the world view as a whole and which is the basis of the religious function of the world view is articulated in a distinct superordinated layer of meaning within the world view. By means of symbolic representations, that layer refers explicitly to a domain of reality that is set apart from the world of everyday life. This domain may be appropriately designated as a sacred cosmos. The symbols which represent the reality of the sacred cosmos may be termed religious representations because they perform, in a specific and concentrated way, the broad religious function of the world view as a whole. The world view in its totality was defined earlier as a universal and nonspecific social form of religion. Consequently, the configuration of religious representations that form *a sacred universe* is to be defined as a *specific historical social form of religion*.

The sacred cosmos is part of the world view. It is socially objectivated in the same manner as the world view as a whole, the special symbolic quality of religious representations notwithstanding. This means that the sacred cosmos forms part of the objective social reality without requiring a distinct and specialized institutional basis. As part of the world view, the sacred cosmos stands in a relationship with the social structure as a whole. The sacred cosmos permeates the various, more or less clearly differentiated, institutional areas such as kinship, the division of labor, and the regulation of the exercise of power. The sacred cosmos determines directly the entire socialization of the individual and is relevant for the total individual biography. To put it differently, religious representations serve to legitimate conduct in the full range of social situations.

Without analyzing in detail the social-structural conditions for the elaboration and maintenance of a sacred cosmos (cf. Swanson 1960; Berger & Luckmann

1966: 107–118) it can be observed generally that this social form of religion predominates in *relatively* "simple" societies. With this term, we refer to societies with a low degree of institutional differentiation – more precisely, with a low degree of "autonomy" of separate institutional areas (roughly corresponding to what is referred to as "primitive fusion" by Redfield) – and a relatively homogeneous social distribution of the world view. In such societies, the sacred cosmos is, in principle, equally accessible to all members of society and equally relevant to them. Since a genuinely homogeneous distribution of the world view is inconceivable, it is obvious that the equal accessibility and relevance of the sacred cosmos is in fact only approximated. No matter how "simple" a society is, it is characterized by some social differentiation, even if that differentiation is primarily institutionalized and articulated in terms of the kinship system. Whatever differentiation there is, it can, and typically does, serve as a basis for an unequal distribution not only of the other elements of the world view but also of the sacred cosmos.

We may say, nonetheless, that the sacred cosmos is a social form of religion which is characterized by segregation of specifically religious representations within the world view *without* specialization of an institutional basis for these representations. The sacred cosmos penetrates, perhaps in varying degrees, the relatively undifferentiated institutional spheres. The maintenance of the sacred cosmos as a social reality and its transmission from generation to generation depend upon general rather than institutionally specialized social processes.

The more "complex" a society, the more likely is it to develop distinct institutions supporting the objectivity and social validity of the sacred cosmos. Full specialization of an institutional basis for the sacred cosmos presupposes, however, a concurrence of circumstances that is historically unique. In relatively "simple" societies, one may already find an incipient differentiation of social roles that are directly linked to the sacred cosmos. In the so-called higher civilizations, the sacred cosmos generally rests on institutions that are at least partly differentiated from kinship institutions and the institutions regulating the exercise of power and the production and distribution of goods and services. Thus the classical civilizations of the Orient, Europe, and the Americas are characterized by some form of institutionalized priesthood. Complete institutional specialization and "autonomy" of religion, with all their structural concomitants, however, emerged only in the Judeo-Christian tradition of Western history. A somewhat remote parallel can be discerned in the Islamic world. Because we are understandably predisposed to identify institutionally specialized religion with religion *tout court*, it is important to stress the fact that the full development of this social form of religion presupposed an intricate pattern of structural and intellectual conditions.

A society can have a world view with a more or less clearly articulated sacred cosmos without having, at the same time, a special institutional basis that carries that cosmos. The establishment of specialized religious institutions, on the other hand, presupposes some degree of articulation of a sacred cosmos in the world view. Generally speaking, one may say that the more pronounced the distinctness of the sacred cosmos, the likelier is the emergence of a specialized institutional basis for that cosmos.

The relation between the sacred cosmos as part of the world view and specialized religious institutions is not one-sided, however. An incipient differentiation of religious institutions as, for example, the emergence of a priesthood, favors and accelerates the segregation of specifically religious representations. Some events in the life of the group, such as the death of a chief, or in the life of the individual, the first hunt, are, of course, apprehended in all societies as having a distinctly higher significance than, for example, the routine planting of coconut trees or the ninety-seventh hunt. Nevertheless, the sharper such dis-stinctions of significance (that is, the more clearly articulated the sacred cosmos), the greater is the likelihood that the events involved, and the knowledge appropriate to deal with such events, will be in charge of relatively specialized social roles. Conversely, the specialization of social roles that are directly linked to the sacred universe will enhance the division of reality into a sacred cosmos and a world of ordinary affairs and the segregation of religious representations from other fields of significance within the world view. Whereas the original articulation of the sacred cosmos does not, in principle, depend on institutional specialization, the formation of specifically religious social roles does presuppose the existence of an articulated sacred cosmos. General recognition of the special status of religious representations in the world view and specialization of religious roles in the social structure do, however, in fact support one another.

The articulation of a sacred cosmos in the world view is, therefore, a necessary but not a sufficient condition for institutional specialization of religion. In addition to this "cultural" prerequisite, several structural conditions must be met before a development toward institutional specialization of religion can set in. Differentiation of social roles whose specific and more or less exclusive task is the administration of knowledge and regulation of performances pertaining to the sacred universe can occur only in societies that fulfill the minimal *general* presuppositions for the evolution of a "complex" social structure. The technology of production and the division of labor must be sufficiently developed to permit the accumulation of surplus over the subsistence minimum. The surplus over the subsistence minimum, in turn, must be large enough to support further differentiation in the division of labor and to permit, more specifically, the growth of specialized bodies of experts.[15] It should be noted, of course, that no matter how "simple" a society, different social roles carry a graduated charge of sacred significance. Thus, for example, fathers may be closer to things sacred than sons – but sons normally become fathers themselves. Or, to give another example, chiefs may possess a sacred quality that is not shared by the other members of the tribe – but chiefs perform many tasks that are only indirectly connected with the sacred cosmos. One may speak here of a preferential distribution of sacred qualities to social roles, but not of specialized religious roles. The sacred qualities remain integrated into the biographical cycle and are "fused" into the over-all role pattern. From such a state of affairs fully specialized religious roles are likely to develop only if the structural conditions presupposed in the removal of full-time "experts" from production are met.

A point that is closely related to the one just made concerns the circumstances surrounding the emergence of religious "theory." Increasing complexity of the division of labor, a large surplus over the subsistence minimum and a correspondingly more differentiated pattern of social stratification combine to produce an increasingly more heterogeneous social distribution of the world view. This means, among other things, that certain types of knowledge will be available only to socially designated experts. It means further that religious representations will be distributed in a pattern of growing inequality. Because of the place and function of the sacred cosmos in the world view, "everybody" will still participate, of course, in some manner in the configuration of religious representations long after other types of knowledge have become reserved for specialists. Thus, for example, the fisherman will know little of bow-making and the bow-maker little of fishing while both will share sacred knowledge although that knowledge may be inferior to that of the chief in degree. The systems of relevance attached to occupational roles, however, are likely to accentuate such differences in sacred knowledge. At a certain level of complexity of the social structure, the social and occupational stratification leads to typical differences in socialization which also affect the acquisition of sacred knowledge. The resulting inequality in the distribution of religious representations will induce, at the very least, the consolidation of different versions of the sacred cosmos among occupational groups and social strata.

The more unequal the distribution of religious representations, the more is the integrating function of the sacred cosmos for the society as a whole threatened. This threat is countered by two mutually not exclusive procedures. The different versions of the sacred cosmos are standardized into an obligatory doctrine, and the existence of whatever differences in religious representations that may remain is explained by an account that is plausible in terms of the inner logic of the sacred cosmos. Now the problems that may lead to the codification of doctrine and the reinforcement of the plausibility of the sacred cosmos do not equally affect all members of a society. The problems arise most often in the transmission of the sacred cosmos from one generation to the next and in situations involving the incumbents of social roles that are charged with a relatively high degree of sacred significance. Such problems are much less likely to arise as long as religious representations are distributed in society in a fairly homogeneous fashion. The "logic" underlying the sacred cosmos is taken for granted because it is equally applicable to different social situations. The validity of that "logic" is reinforced by everybody. Thus the sacred cosmos and its underlying logic remain unproblematic. The chance of situations occurring in which the "logic" of the sacred universe is no longer self-explanatory increases, however, as the social distribution of religious representations grows more heterogeneous.

Especially, those involved in the transmission of the sacred universe to the next generation and the incumbents of social roles containing a relatively high degree of sacred significance are likely to find that the sacred cosmos and its "logic" require some elaboration in order to retain their plausibility. Thus the relation of religious representations to one another becomes the topic of more or less systematic reflection and interpretation. The meaningful coherence of the world view as a whole and of the sacred cosmos is worked out "theoretically" by a body of incipient experts. If these experts can be set aside from the production process, institutional specialization of religious "theory" proceeds apace. In sum, the structurally determined growth of codification and interpretation of the sacred cosmos significantly contributes to the differentiation of specialized religious roles.

It should be noted briefly that "extrinsic" factors may also encourage reflection about and systematic interpretation of a sacred cosmos. Thus, for example, the contact of different cultures typically produces situations in which the homegrown variety of a sacred universe confronts an imported religion. Such situations encourage "theoretical" efforts proving the superiority of the native religion or syncretizing the native and the imported religions in some way. More often than not this strengthens the trend toward institutional specialization of religion by provoking the establishment of defensive organizations of an incipiently ecclesiastic type.

With increasing specialization of religious roles, laymen come to participate less and less directly in the sacred cosmos. Only the religious experts are in "full" possession of sacred knowledge. The application of that knowledge is the province of the experts and the laymen rely increasingly on the mediation of the experts in their relations with the sacred universe.

If religiously relevant conduct originally rests on fully internalized norms and general social controls, conformity in such matters is increasingly supervised by religious specialists in more "complex" societies. While religious representations originally served to legitimate conduct in all kinds of situations, increasing specialization of religion results in the transfer of social controls over "religious behavior" to specific institutions. The vested interests of religious experts in the recruitment and training of their successors, in the exclusion of laymen from the "higher" forms of sacred knowledge, and in the defense of privileges against competing bodies of experts typically lead to the formation of some kind of "ecclesiastic" organization (cf. Wach 1944: esp. 4, 5).

Institutional specialization as a *social form of religion*, we may say in summary, is characterized by standardization of the sacred cosmos in a well-defined doctrine, differentiation of fulltime religious roles, transfer of sanctions enforcing doctrinal and ritual conformity to special agencies, and the emergence of organizations of the "ecclesiastic" type.

Only if religion is localized in special social institutions does an antithesis between "religion" and "society" develop. Such localization is the necessary condition for the history of religious dogma and ecclesiastic organization as distinct from secular culture and "social," that is, nonreligious institutions. The history of the so-called higher civilizations shows a wide range of relationships between "religion" and "society" ranging from accommodation to conflict. Not only does the degree of institutional specialization of religion vary in these civilizations but also the position which religious institutions occupy in the social structure as a whole. Correspondingly, the antithesis between "religion" and "society" is etched sharply into the history of some of these societies while it remains in abeyance in others.

Religion originally serves in the integration of the social order and in the legitimation of the *status quo*. Institutionally specialized religion may become, however, a dynamic social force in some historical circumstances. Once the sacred universe and the "world" develop their own "logic" and once the latter is backed up by different institutions, tensions may develop between religious experience and the requirements of everyday affairs. Specifically religious communities may emerge, claiming loyalties that place their followers in conflict with "secular" institutions – or the members of other religious communities. The history of Christianity – also of Islam and Buddhism – documents a variety of attempts to find intellectual and structural solutions to such tensions and conflicts. These observations do not imply, of course, that institutionally specialized religion is an intrinsically "progressive" force. If anything, the opposite is true. But in contrast to other social forms of religion, institutional specialization of religion always contains the possibility of an antithesis between "religion" and "society." The latter may act as a catalyst of social change.

It should be noted again that institutional specialization of religion can be approximated in various degrees. The existence of a part-time priesthood, for example, may mark an incipient stage of institutional specialization. Theocracies may be considered an intermediate form of institutional specialization. The church in the Judeo-Christian tradition of Western history, however, represents an extreme and historically unique case of institutional specialization of religion. It emerges from an extraordinarily sharp segregation of the sacred cosmos from the profane world in Hebrew theology, formulation of the inner logic of that cosmos in eschatological terms, heterogeneity of the world views, "culture conflicts" and syncretism in the areas in which Christianity arose, a fairly high degree of "autonomy" of political and economic institutions in the Roman Empire, etc. The institutionalization of doctrine, the development of ecclesiastic organization, and the differentiation of a religious community from society at large reached a degree that was not paralleled elsewhere. It should be also remembered, however, that in all societies characterized by this social form of religion, even if to a lesser degree, the segregation of the sacred cosmos in the world view is matched, to some extent, by specialization of religious roles in the social structure and by the existence of groups claiming a distinctly religious quality.

Notes

13 Cf. von Humboldt 1953, pp. 463–473. It is interesting to note that Humboldt was clearly aware of the objective and objectivating character of language: "At the same time that language has a character that is indeed internal, it also exists as an independent and external fact which exerts' constraint on man." (*Op. cit.* p. 392; my translation). The sociologist must be struck by the fact that this statement about language enumerates the criteria by which Durkheim, in his *Rules of the Sociological* Method much later defined a social fact.

14 From the large and steadily increasing literature on the subject we refer only, in addition to Humboldt, to Benjamin Lee Whorf 1956, esp. the essay, "Languages and Logic," pp. 233–246, without wishing to enter here the debate on the validity of the linguistic "determinism" hypothesis (Cf. Hoijer 1954). On the general problems of the sociology of language see Luckmann 1969.

15 We are touching here upon some basic problems of the sociology of knowledge which it is impossible to discuss here in detail. Cf. Berger & Luckmann 1966.

V

INDIVIDUAL RELIGIOSITY

Religion is rooted in a basic anthropological fact: the transcendence of biological nature by human organisms. The individual human potential for transcendence is realized, originally, in social processes that rest on the reciprocity of face-to-face situations. These processes lead to the construction of objective world views, the articulation of sacred universes and, under certain circumstances, to institutional specialization of religion. The social forms of religion are thus based on what is, in a certain sense, an individual religious phenomenon: the individuation of consciousness and conscience in the matrix of human intersubjectivity.

The concrete historical individual, of course, does not go about constructing world views and sacred universes. He is born into a pre-existing society and into a prefabricated world view. He does not, therefore, achieve the status of a human person in genuinely original acts of transcendence. Humanity, as a reality that transcends biological nature, is pre-established for him in the social forms of religion. The individuation of consciousness and conscience of historical individuals is objectively determined by historical religions in one of their social forms.

A world view is an objective and stable social fact for the human organism born into a society. It is transmitted to him by concrete fellow men who demonstrate and validate its objectivity in a variety of social situations and reinforce its stability in continuous social processes. The world view is an objective system of meaning by which an individual past and future are integrated into a coherent biography and in which the emergent person locates himself in relation to fellow men, the social order, and the transcendent sacred universe. The continuity of sense in individual life is dependent on the coherence of meaning in the world view.

DOI: 10.4324/9781003257875-6

In the process of socialization, a historical world view is internalized. The objective system of meaning is transformed into a subjective reality. This means that the interpretive schemes and models of conduct that are objectivated in the world view are superimposed on the subjective stream of consciousness. It also means that the hierarchy of significance underlying a world view becomes a subjective system of relevance. In accordance with this system, the individual apprehends his experiences in a graduated pattern of importance. In accordance with that system, a pattern of priorities consolidates for the individual which designates some actions as more urgent than others. An objective world view becomes a subjective system of orientation in "objective" reality.

Just as the hierarchy of significance underlying a world view need not be articulated explicitly but may remain a purely "structural" trait of the world view, the subjective system of relevance need not be something that the individual can consciously apprehend as a system. He may merely apprehend specific interpretive schemes and specific motives. Nonetheless the subjective system of relevance is a constitutive element of personal identity by virtue of the fact that it manifests itself consistently as a pattern of priorities in the individual's choices among alternative courses of action.

We may say, in sum, that the individuation of consciousness and conscience occurs for historical individuals in the internalization of an already constructed world view rather than in the original creation of world views. The world view with its underlying hierarchy of significance becomes an individual system of relevance that is superimposed on the stream of consciousness. It is a constitutive element of personal identity. The personal identity of a historical individual is, thus, the subjective expression of the objective significance of a historical world view. Earlier we defined the world view as a universal social form of religion. Correspondingly, we may now define personal identity as a universal form of individual religiosity.

Within the world view, a sacred cosmos that represents symbolically the hierarchy of significance underlying the world view may become articulated. If an individual is born into a society in which a sacred cosmos forms part of objective reality, the individual will internalize the sacred cosmos in the form of specific religious representations. The internalized religious representations retain, of course, their reference to an objective sacred cosmos and are characterized, among the other internalized interpretive schemes and models of conduct, by a status of extraordinary significance. They are segregated within the total field of consciousness as a more or less distinct stratum of meanings. These meanings illuminate, for the individual, the routine of everyday life and instill sense into the brute finality of life's crises. Both the routine and the crises of individual life are placed by means of the internalized religious representations into a transcendent context of meaning and are legitimated by the "logic" of the sacred cosmos. The internalized religious representations thus form a subjective system of "ultimate" relevance and overarching motives.

This "religious" layer of individual consciousness stands in a relation to personal identity that is analogous to the relation of the sacred cosmos to the world view as a whole. In other words, the subjective system of "ultimate" relevance – always retaining its reference to the objective sacred cosmos – serves to legitimate and justify explicitly the subjective pattern of priorities that is a constitutive element of personal identity.

The more clearly articulated the sacred cosmos within the world view, the more likely is it that the internalized religious representations will form a relatively distinct "religious" stratum in the consciousness of individuals socialized into that world view. This implies that – other things being equal – such individuals will be more likely to be able to formulate matters of "ultimate" relevance in explicit terms for themselves and for others. The communication of distinctly religious experiences, in turn, will tend to reinforce the segregation of the sacred cosmos in the world view. It should be remembered, however, that neither the world view as a whole nor the sacred cosmos are internalized merely as a series of concepts and symbols but as configurations of meaning that determine the subjective pattern of priorities. By means of that pattern they become an effective part of personal identity even if the rhetoric of "ultimate" justifications is not fully articulated. If a sacred cosmos is internalized in a distinctly "religious" layer of individual consciousness, we may speak of a form of individual religiosity that is more specific than personal identity as such.

Since, as was noted earlier, the sacred cosmos is embedded in the social structure, the individual encounters in the course of primary socialization (and later) many social situations in which the religious representations – about to be internalized – are reinforced by various institutions which are not specialized in religious matters. Norms endowed with sacred significance, for example, father, chivalry, caste, my country – to choose a few examples at random – are effective in different institutional contexts. In these contexts, the concrete application of the internalized religious representations is defined. Because it is so defined by institutions that are not specifically religious, the religious representations are likely to retain their general and superordinated significance in spite of the fact that they are internalized in a distinct layer of individual consciousness. As we shall see presently, church-oriented religiosity contains the possibility of a divergent development.

As indicated before, full institutional specialization of religion occurs only under particular socio-historic circumstances. In societies in which religion does take on this social form, it is taken for granted that religion is mediated by the church, just as it is taken for granted in other societies that religion is identical with the social form in which it appears. The complications which arise as a result of so-called secularization we shall discuss later. The individual is brought up in a situation in which religion constitutes a coherent system of meaning which refers to a symbolic reality that is recognized by everybody as religious and which is represented in society by men, buildings, procedures, and so forth whose religious quality is clearly marked. The formation of individual religiosity is necessarily determined by the ready-made "official" model of religion. The degree of restraint which the "official" model exerts on the development of individual religiosity is, however, variable within certain limits. This is one of the points that will have to be taken up again in the discussion of so-called secularization. Before the onset of secularization, however, the typical processes of socialization lead – in societies characterized by this social form of religion – to the development of individual religiosity in the forms of church-oriented religiosity. For the typical member of such societies, matters of "ultimate" significance are, therefore, those which are designated as religious by the specialized religious institutions in their "official" model.

Individual religiosity is thus concretely shaped by a historical church. The sacred cosmos is available in the form of a doctrine which is codified in sacred texts and commentaries. The doctrine is transmitted and interpreted by an official body of experts in a manner that is binding for the laymen. All performances that are directly related to the sacred cosmos are fixed in a liturgy which is enacted by appointed specialists or under their supervision and control. Furthermore, the church, like any historical institution, develops traditions which are rooted in the self-conceptions and vested interests of administrative bureaucracies and power elites. Although these traditions have little connection with the sacred cosmos, ecclesiastic bodies are in the advantageous position of being able to legitimate them in terms that are concordant with the "logic" of the sacred cosmos – as interpreted by them. Religion becomes a circumscribed and eminently visible part of social reality which includes not only founders, prophets, sacred texts, theologians, and rituals but also buildings, Sunday schools, fund raisers and church tax collectors, ministers' wives, and sextons.

The fact that individual religiosity is shaped by a highly specialized social institution has some important consequences. The relations that link the individual to the sacred cosmos are defined by an institution that claims the exclusive right to interpret matters of "ultimate" significance and pursues, at the same time, various "secular" aims which are determined by the organizational structure of the institution, the relations of conflict or accommodation to other specialized institutions, the vested interests of its body of experts, and so forth. It was noted before that the configuration of religious representations is internalized by the individual as a subjective system of "ultimate" relevance. In societies characterized by institutional specialization of religion, this means concretely that the individual is socialized into the "official" model of religion with the express purpose that this model may constitute his system of "ultimate" significance. The successful accomplishment of this purpose presupposes, however, that the "official" model is coherent in a manner that is subjectively plausible. If this is the case, the internalized "official" model retains its general and superordinated significance in the life of the individual; that is, it is capable of integrating and legitimating the interpretive schemes and norms of conduct that govern the routines and the crises of his existence. In institutionally specialized religion, however, the sense-coherence and the subjective plausibility of the "official" model are endangered by three closely related difficulties which do not arise jointly in other social forms of religion.

First, the "official" model of religion does not only include articulations of the sacred cosmos and definitions of procedures for dealing with the sacred cosmos but also interpretations of the role of the church (and the religious experts) in the relations of the individual to the sacred cosmos *and* to other social institutions. The "official" model is, of course, formulated and elaborated by the experts and the various dimensions of the "official" model eventually become the subject of specialized knowledge, such as doctrine, liturgy, "social ethics," and so forth. The – relative – distinctness of various dimensions in the "official" model is reflected to some extent in the processes by which the individual is socialized into the "official" model. Consequently, individual church-oriented religiosity contains psychologically more or less segregated modalities which are the subjective correlates of the dimensions of the "official" model. An approved doctrine finds its subjective correlate in a set of individual beliefs. A standardized liturgy has its subjective correlate in a circumscribed pattern of individual observances. The traditions of the church as a historical institution find subjective correlates in various forms of individual identification with ecclesiastic bodies, religious groups and communities, and in "secular" activities performed by the individual consciously and explicitly as a church member (cf. Fichter 1951; Fichter 1954; Luckmann 1959a; Luckmann 1959b).

The modalities of church-oriented religiosity *may* continue to form a subjectively meaningful whole. The "proper" relation of the modalities is built into the "official" model more or less explicitly, for example, as an emphasis on "faith," or on "good works," or on ritual correctness. This relation is, therefore, also capable of internalization along with the specific dimensions of the "official" model. The consolidation of distinct dimensions in the "official" model is not a sufficient cause for the dissolution of the sense-coherence of church-oriented religiosity. It does represent, however, a *potential* danger to the subjective plausibility of the "official" model as a subjective system of "ultimate" significance.

A second trait of institutionally specialized religion contributes to this danger. The "official" model is formulated as a set of highly specific norms of performance and belief. The segregation of the sacred cosmos from the "world" could encourage a weakening of the integrating function of religious representations for everyday conduct if the effect of that segregation were not counteracted by the pervasiveness of religion in society. The pervasiveness of religion, in turn, results from the fact that the sacred cosmos has a general rather than a specialized social basis. In the case of institutionally specialized religion, however, nothing counteracts the psychological effects of the segregation of the sacred cosmos. On the contrary, religious representations are formulated as highly specific norms of performance and belief that are attached to discontinuous role performances.

"Religion" may be, therefore, apprehended by the individual as the fulfillment of *particular* requirements. The consolidation of psychologically distinct modalities of church-oriented religiosity obviously supports this possibility. The fulfillment of role requirements is, in general, capable of a high degree of routinization. Religious role requirements are no exception. Specific religious norms such as Easter Duty, belief in a Trinitarian God and observance of the Sabbath can be, consequently, fulfilled as a matter of routine, in more or less segregated blocks of action and "opinion." In that case, the original relationship of the institutionalized religious norms to the subjective system of "ultimate" significance is threatened, although the sacred quality of the norms may continue to be nominally recognized. The *effective* system of subjective priorities may become divorced from matters that are defined as being of "ultimate" significance in the "official" model. The rhetoric of the internalized "official" model may be still plausible enough to motivate the fulfillment of specific religious norms. Under certain circumstances – which we shall have to discuss later – the plausibility of that rhetoric may decrease to such an extent that the institutionalized requirements are no longer fulfilled by the typical members of society – unless "nonreligious" motives are substituted for "religious" ones. In general, we may say that institutionally specialized religion is characterized by a certain precariousness of the corresponding form of individual religiosity. Matters of "ultimate" significance, as defined in the *official* model, are potentially convertible into routinized and discontinuous observances (or approximate observances or nonobservance) of specific religious requirements whose sacred quality may become merely nominal. Thus the specifically religious representations may cease to function as integrating elements of the *subjective* system of "ultimate" significance.

The subjective plausibility of the "official" model of religion meets a third difficulty in another trait that is characteristic of this social form of religion. The "official" model is formulated, transmitted, and interpreted by a specialized group of "fulltime" experts. Even if the experts are not entirely segregated from the world of everyday life as it is typically encountered by the other members of society, they are primarily involved in matters related to the sacred cosmos, in "theory" and in the administration of a specialized institution. They may, therefore, become divorced, to some extent, from the typical routines and crises of the laymen. This represents a potential danger to the congruence of the sacred cosmos of the experts and matters of great, if not of "ultimate," significance for the laymen. No doubt this danger can be countered more or less effectively by explicit "pedagogical" procedures as, for example, by the translation of the sacred cosmos of the "theologians" into the language of the laymen by a body of "pastoral" specialists. Even if differentiated versions of the sacred cosmos develop, a flexible ecclesiastic organization may manage to integrate them in a common conception. Nonetheless, the "theoretical" character of the "official" model of religion contributes to the potential divergence between that model and the subjective system of "ultimate" significance of the typical members of a society. Combined with the consolidation of psychologically distinct modalities of church-oriented religiosity and the routinization of the fulfillment of highly specific religious norms, it is an important factor in the genesis of so-called secularization.

VI

RELIGION AND PERSONAL IDENTITY IN MODERN SOCIETY

At the beginning of this essay we asked a number of questions about the relation of an individual's life to the social order in the modern world. How does an individual today typically apprehend his relation to society? What are the social conditions for the subjectively apprehended sense of individual existence in the modern industrial societies? Having formulated these questions, we noted that the general problem of the relation of the individual to the social order *and* the specific articulation of this problem in modern society were recognized as "religious" by Weber as well as Durkheim and that, consequently, a theory of religion occupied a prominent place in their sociological work. It seemed promising to approach our questions by developing some implications of their respective positions and to start out with the assumption that religion would reflect the impact of modern society on individual existence. It became apparent that for an analysis of contemporary religion under this perspective, the recent sociology of religion proved of little help. The reason for that could be easily found in the fact that the recent sociology of religion tends to take a particular historical form for the prototype of religion *tout court*. Under that assumption, research on church and church religion in industrial societies simply seemed to prove that religion was generally declining, that the contemporary world was becoming increasingly less "religious," and that the typical citizen of the modern world was leading a life which was increasingly lacking in "genuine" significance.

In order to find meaningful answers to our initial questions, it seemed necessary to find a perspective on religion in contemporary society that was less prejudiced and parochial. We investigated, therefore, the anthropological condition for religion and described the development of various social forms of religion from that condition. Our analysis was to discover the common elements or, as we may

DOI: 10.4324/9781003257875-7

say, the underlying religious function in the historical articulations of religion, as well as the structural determinants of the main social forms of such articulations. A brief summary of the results of this analysis may prove helpful at this point.

The anthropological condition of religion is to be found in the "dialectics" of individual and society that pervade the processes in which consciousness and conscience are individuated. These processes lead to the objectivation of a world view which functions as a "transcendent" hierarchy of meaning *vis-à-vis* the immanently "unbound" subjective stream of consciousness. We defined, therefore, the world view as a universal but nonspecific social form of religion. Its subjective correlate is to be found in the internalized system of relevance which forms the basis of a personal identity. Our analysis uncovered the conditions under which specific social forms of religion emerge from that universal form. In the universal form, the religious function is diffused in society. It is increasingly concentrated in the specific social forms which range from an articulation of a sacred cosmos in the world view to full institutional specialization of religion. The subjective correlate of the former is to be found in the internal segregation of religious representations in the form of an individual system of "ultimate" relevance. The subjective correlate of the latter is to be found in the configuration of internalized dimensions of the "official" model of religion, a configuration which we called church-oriented religiosity.

An objective world view is, of course, a constitutive element of any society, just as an individual system of relevance is a constitutive element of personal identity. The statement that religion is present in nonspecific form in all societies and all "normal" (socialized) individuals is, therefore, axiomatic. It specifies a religious dimension in the "definition" of individual and society but is empty of specific empirical content.

It is an empirical question, however, whether societies exist, in fact, which have religion *only* in this nonspecific form. At this point, we need merely say that the existence of such societies is conceivable, just as one can conceive, in analogy, of individuals who act according to a pattern of priorities without being able to articulate "ultimate" reasons for their conduct. For the problem at hand, another empirical question is more pertinent and we shall have to discuss it in some detail. If a society is characterized by an institutionally specialized social form of religion, what are the consequences for the religious function embodied in that form? Given the institutional character of religion it would be unrealistic to assume that this social form would stand in a simple relation to the universal and nonspecific social form of religion. In a sense, the church is more, and less, than the "perfect" historical articulation of a sacred cosmos that represents the hierarchy of meaning in a world view.

We may approach this problem by first imagining a situation of complete identity between church, sacred cosmos, and the hierarchy of meaning in the world view. On the level of subjective correlates this implies complete identity between the "official" model of religion, the individual system of "ultimate" significance, and the individual pattern of priorities. It may be noted in passing that this situation conforms to what seems to be an implicit theological ideal. This situation cannot be fully realized; it is empirically impossible for reasons to which we alluded in a previous context of analysis and which we shall have to discuss fully in a moment. At best, this imaginary situation may serve as a starting point for the construction of an "ideal type," a heuristic model for the comparison of different phases in the institutional specialization of religion. It is apparent that this situation was approximated to a higher degree in the Christian societies of the Middle Ages than in more recent Western history.

The notion of complete congruence between the "official" model of religion and the subjective system of "ultimate" significance implicitly rests on the assumption of "perfect" socialization of an individual into the social order. This assumption is, of course, untenable. Nonetheless, it might be possible to disregard this difficulty in the case of relatively simple societies in which individuals typically internalize "most" of a relatively homogeneous culture. It would be entirely unrealistic to disregard this difficulty in the case of more complex societies. It is precisely in such societies, however, that religion is likely to become institutionally specialized. In other words, one might postulate a fairly high degree of congruence between the sacred cosmos and the internalized system of "ultimate" significance for the members of relatively simple societies. One cannot postulate a similarly high degree of congruence between the "official" model of religion and the subjective system of "ultimate" significance for members of societies in which institutional specialization of religion has occurred.

Our construction of a situation in which complete identity prevails between church, sacred cosmos, and the hierarchy of significance of the world view is unrealistic for another reason. Fully specialized religious institutions arise only under conditions of considerable complexity in the social structure, including a heterogeneous social distribution of the world view. Such institutions cannot, therefore, express *the* hierarchy of meaning in *the* world view. In societies in which this would be conceivable, on the other hand, the conditions for full institutional specialization of religion are absent.

An additional factor that must be considered is the rise of competing sacred universes in societies in which the structural conditions favor the development of institutional specialization of religion. But even if we neglect, for the moment, the consequences of religious "pluralism" for specialized religious institutions, we may conclude that the conditions for full institutional specialization of religion and the presuppositions for complete congruence between the "official" model and individual religiosity are mutually exclusive.

Institutional specialization of religion transforms the relation of the individual to the sacred cosmos *and* to the social order in general. As a result of this transformation, the church becomes an ambivalent phenomenon with respect to its religious function. The church enters into manifold relations with other more or less specialized institutions whose primary functions are "secular." The relations of the church to political and economic institutions range from mutual support to partial accommodation to competition to open conflict. In the context of such relations, the church inevitably develops "secular" interests of its own. In addition to a doctrinal and liturgical tradition, an economic, political, and administrative tradition of the church is formed. The latter has considerable weight in the day-to-day handling of the "secular" institutional problems that confront the church as a going concern. These traditions "compromise" the purposes for which the church was "designed" in the understanding of those who take the specifically religious claims of the church at face value, to an extent that remains to be discussed.

The religious experts soon come to recognize that the ambivalence of the church with respect to its religious function represents a serious problem. If they take the "official" model of religion at face value, they may find the "secular" operations of the church scandalous or, at least, problematic to an extent that requires legitimation of these operations in terms which are consistent with the "logic" of the sacred universe. In any case, the religious experts are professionally obligated to deal with the social-psychological consequences of this problem. The plausibility of the "official" model of religion is potentially endangered by the "secular" operations of the church. In transmitting the "official" model to the laity, the religious experts must, therefore, supply "sacred" explanations for the "secular" activities of the church. The plausibility of the "official" model is threatened most acutely in a "pluralistic" situation. The partisans of sacred universes that are competing for "official" status put forth claims to "doctrinal" superiority; typically they also claim a higher degree of "purity" from "secular" involvements for themselves. The history of sectarian movements in Christianity and Islam offers ample support for this observation. In general, we may say that the ambivalence of the church is most likely to be recognized as a problem whenever the plausibility of the "official" model of religion is threatened for additional, "external" reasons. Recognition of the problem inspires theoretical efforts of the religious experts to find "sacred" explanations for the "secular" involvement. The doctrine of the visible and invisible church in Christian theology may serve as an example. The success of the theoretical efforts to safeguard the plausibility of the "official" model depends on a variety of factors. Most important are the flexibility of the "logic" of the respective sacred universe and the effective monopoly a given body of religious experts have in the propagation of their "official" model. The root of the problem, however, cannot be eradicated by theoretical efforts: the church, as a concrete institution, cannot remain exclusively determined by its religious function.

Another consequence of institutional specialization of religion is that the incongruence between the "official" model of religion and the socially predominant individual systems of "ultimate" significance may reach critical proportions.

A sacred cosmos is, of course, a relatively stable part of social reality even before religion is institutionally specialized. Whenever matters of "ultimate" significance are objectivated in a world view that transcends subjective processes and individual biographies, they become more resistant to change than everyday affairs whose meaning occupies a subordinate position in the hierarchy of significance. Institutional specialization of religion which includes standardized transmission of the "official" model, a doctrinal canon and controls against deviation, decisively reinforces the "textual" stability of the sacred cosmos. The consolidation of religious beliefs and practices in an "official" model and the institutional support of that model bestow a high degree of objectivity and continuity on matters that are presumed to be of "ultimate" significance to everybody. The stability of the sacred cosmos is, furthermore, one of the most important vested interests of the influential body of religious experts.

Here a problem arises. It can be postulated that a high degree of stability of the sacred cosmos supports the stability of relatively simple societies – at the same time that it reflects such stability. On the other hand, institutional specialization of religion and the correspondingly reinforced stability of the sacred cosmos characterize societies with a relatively complex social structure. Such societies, however, have rates of social change that are, at least, moderate. Even a moderate rate of social change implies that the routines and the problems of everyday life of the individuals in such societies vary over the generations. Under conditions of rapid social change, the problem becomes still more acute. The everyday concerns of the fathers are no longer those of the sons and many of the concerns of the sons were unknown to the fathers. In the context of such changing concerns, even the major and "invariable" biographical crises and their solutions, including death, will appear in a different perspective to the sons. In general, we may say that matters that come to be of "ultimate" significance for the members of later generations are likely to be congruent only to a limited extent with matters that were of "ultimate" significance to earlier generations. The latter, however, were "frozen" in sacred texts, doctrines and rituals. A serious problem of institutional specialization of religion consists, therefore, in the fact that the "official" model of religion changes at a slower rate than the "objective" social conditions that codetermine the predominant individual systems of "ultimate" significance.

It should be noted, however, that several factors counteract or, at least, retard the growing incongruence between the "official" model and individual religiosity. It is difficult to imagine circumstances under which the "official" model could remain completely inflexible. The religious experts are professionally motivated to defend the religious *status quo*. They are also motivated to transmit *successfully* the "official" model of religion to the laymen. The religious experts may succeed in isolating themselves from the "world" to some extent and thereby avoid the full effect, on their own lives, of the processes which transform the lives of the laymen. Nevertheless, they cannot avoid noting the growing difficulties in making the "official" model plausible to the layman whose everyday world no longer has a compelling relation to the traditional sacred cosmos. At the very least, the religious experts will be forced to recognize some incongruity between "ideals" and "facts." Unless the religious experts retreat into enclaves in which the "ideals" remain uncontested and plausible – and effectively abdicate from their "official" position – they will readjust the "official" model to the requirements of changing conditions. The areas in which such readjustments become necessary are typically defined, *post hoc*, as marginal to the doctrinal core. This procedure permits considerable flexibility. Because religion is institutionally specialized and the sacred cosmos develops a doctrinal history, however, there are both "textual" and organizational limitations to the procedure. The danger that specifically religious representations which are "frozen" as catechismal items lose some or much plausibility as subjective systems of "ultimate" significance is, therefore, only partly obviated.

The potential incongruence between the "official" model of religion and individual religiosity is counteracted by another set of circumstances. Let us assume that the "official" model remains fairly stable while the everyday life of successive generations is "objectively" transformed by social change. The members of successive generations are thus socialized into the *same* "official" model of religion. They find matters of "ultimate" significance predefined in that model. The "objective" processes that would tend to modify the subjective systems of "ultimate" significance of the adult members of the changing society, exert only an indirect influence on the children in the earlier phases of socialization. While the adults are involved in the affairs of everyday life that are determined by the changing character of "secular" institutions, the children are still removed from these affairs. Unless the family actively interferes with the religious socialization of the child – which would presuppose the existence of consolidated counter-ideologies – the child will internalize the "official" model at face value. There is no compelling reason why the child should consciously experience an incongruity between the model and the problems of everyday life. In other words, as long as socialization into the "official" model of religion is general, the typical individual will, at first, accept the "official" definition of matters of "ultimate" significance. Once he has internalized the "official" model, however, he will tend to view matters of everyday life in its categories. He will be slow in gaining awareness of the gap between what is "officially" of "ultimate" significance and what is "objectively" important for him. The internalized "official" model of religion produces a rather generalized attitude which leads to "automatic" resistance to such processes of social change as might increase the irrelevance of the "official" model for the individual, as long as the rhetoric of specifically religious representations remains fairly effective. We may consider this to be one of the reasons why churches, especially established churches, tend to instill a certain amount of general "conservatism" into their members even if the "official" model of religion transmitted by the churches should not include an overt "conservative" ideology.

Another – entirely "unintended" – consequence of institutional specialization of religion is the weakening of the superordinated position of specifically religious representations in the subjective systems of relevance. Before institutional specialization of religion, religious representations occupy a position of "ultimate" significance in individual consciousness. According to the institutionalized "official" model, specifically religious representations are intended to occupy the same position. A problem arises, however, because specialized religious norms are consolidated in circumscribed social roles. This serves to articulate and make socially visible the jurisdiction of religion but, concurrently, to narrow the habitual applicability of religious norms to segregated areas of belief and practice. Performances of specifically religious roles are integrated, in fact, with performances of other, more or less specialized "secular" roles. Leaving out of consideration the special problem of "full-time" experts in religion, specifically religious roles are "part-time" *de facto* if not *de jure*. Performance of the nonreligious roles is determined by the "secular" norms which develop in the more or less autonomous economic and political institutions.[16] The more the traces of a sacred cosmos are eliminated from the "secular" norms, the weaker is the plausibility of the global claim of religious norms. The latter become attached in an increasingly exclusive manner to the "part-time" religious roles. The integration of discontinuous performances of religious and nonreligious roles in a biographical pattern constitutes a potential problem for the individual. The *de facto* integration of performances does not yet provide an integration of the meaning of these performances in overarching biographical categories. It is, of course, one of the "original" functions of religious representations to supply the individual with an "objective" model for a subjectively meaningful integration of conduct in diverse areas of life. As we indicated, however, institutional specialization of religion typically leads to a narrowed jurisdiction of specifically religious representations which, in turn, weakens or destroys the effectiveness of these representations as a model for the integration of sense.

Some individuals may continue to take the global claims of specifically religious representations at face value, despite the circumstances which we found to weaken the plausibility of such claims. If they "naïvely" (the term is not used pejoratively) cling to these claims, the problem of "meaningful integration" is resolved for them by elimination of the inconsistent "secular" elements of the problem. It is apparent that this solution leads to "objective" difficulties and, in the extreme case, to an inability to perform the nonreligious roles effectively and to some form of "martyrdom." More frequently, this "naïve" attitude results in a partial withdrawal from the "world" – accompanied by compromises with the "world" which are defined as tolerable. Various Pietist groups may serve as examples of different degrees of withdrawal and compromise.

For the member of society who habitually attaches "religion" to segregated areas of belief and behavior and who does not "naïvely" cling to the global claim of "religion," a meaningful integration of specifically religious and nonreligious performances and norms with their respective jurisdictional claims remains a problem. The structural determinants of this problem typically motivate the individual to reflect. We are not postulating here a general and systematic process of theoretical thought about the meaning of life and the like. We merely refer to the fact that the conflicting or, at least, disparate requirements of "religion" and the "world" stimulate the individual "to stop and think" occasionally. Such reflection can lead to a variety of solutions. One is a "leap of faith." Superficially this solution resembles the "naïve" attitude previously described. The difference is, however, that here individual religiosity, initially patterned after the "official" model, becomes reconstituted after a phase of "doubt" as a purely individualistic solution to the problems of life. Another "solution" may consist in finding oneself unable to formulate a plausible solution and in returning to a prereflective attitude in which one shifts from "secular" to religious performances in routine fashion. A third possibility lies in the formulation of an explicitly "secular" value system: consequently religious roles are either performed for "opportunistic" reasons or abandoned. A certain amount of reflection is common to these solutions.[17] At various levels of reflection and intellectual consistency, the individual, furthermore, tends to restrict the relevance of specifically religious norms to domains that are not yet pre-empted by the jurisdictional claims of "secular" institutions. Thus, religion becomes a "private affair." We may conclude by saying that institutional specialization of religion, along with the specialization of other institutional areas, starts a development that transforms religion into an increasingly "subjective" and "private" reality. Since this trend culminates in the contemporary situation of religion, we shall have to discuss it in more detail presently.

Before turning to the concrete questions concerning religion in modern society, however, we continue with the discussion of the relation between the "official" model of religion and the individual systems of "ultimate" significance. We have shown that the consequences of institutional specialization of religion make it impossible that full congruence between the two should ever be realized. We indicated, however, that while full congruence is impossible, the continuous growth of incongruence is checked or, at least, retarded by certain factors. We remarked, furthermore, that these factors seem to have become increasingly less effective in the recent history of institutionally specialized religion.

While the assumption of full congruence between the "official" model of religion and the individual systems of "ultimate" significance is unrealistic, the notion of *complete* incongruence between the two leads to a contradiction in terms. Complete incongruence would be conceivable only if no member of a society were socialized into the "official" model. In that case, however, it would be meaningless to continue to speak of an "official" model. What *is* conceivable is that a model of religion that had been "official" for former generations ceases to be "official" for later generations. Thus, for example, one "official" model may be replaced by another. If, however, the old model remains obligatory for part of the population, while another part of the population embraces a new model, both models will be less than fully "official," unless both models receive a socially distinct and circumscribed status (for example, the "official" model for the rulers and the "official" model for the ruled). A genuinely "pluralistic" competition between various models of religion, however, will tend to undermine the "official" status of both. A more interesting possibility is the eventual loss of "official" status by a model of religion without a new "official" model being substituted for it. Such a development signals the end of institutional specialization of religion. Even in this case the former "official" model would not disappear without leaving traces in the world view and the norms of the "secular" institutions governing the everyday lives of the members of later generations. The model would continue to exert an indirect influence on the formation of individual systems of "ultimate" significance long after it had ceased to be "official" in any relevant sense of the term. Other things being equal, this influence would, of course, diminish over the generations. As these considerations indicate, however, it would be unrealistic even then to assume a radical and complete incongruence between a formerly "official" model of religion and individual religiosity.

It is even more obvious that we can conceive only of *relative* incongruence in societies that are still characterized by institutional specialization of religion. Depending on the strength of the factors that foster and those that retard the growth of incongruence, the relation between the "official" model of religion and the prevalent individual systems of "ultimate" significance can approximate but cannot reach either full congruence or complete incongruence. It will be therefore useful to end these formal considerations by discussing briefly some intermediate types.

We need not elaborate on the description of a type that is located in relative proximity to the hypothetical pole of congruence. This type is characterized by the fact that "everybody" is socialized fairly successfully into the "official" model of religion by a slow rate of social change and by some minimal flexibility of the "official" model. Under such conditions, the factors that tend to counteract the growth of incongruence will prevail over the factors that tend to foster a rapid increase of the latter.

If, however, the rate of social change increases without a corresponding increase in the flexibility of the "official" model, a different situation arises. While "everybody" is still socialized into the "official" model, the consequences of the changing "objective" circumstances in the everyday lives of the members of the society will suffice to produce a marked degree of incongruence between the "official" model and the *effectively* prevalent individual systems of priorities. Such incongruence as may develop need not immediately change the individual systems of "ultimate" significance – that is, the internalized "official" model. It is more likely that those who have been successfully socialized into the "official" model will not consciously apprehend the changes in their *effective* priorities. In other words, while the changing "objective" circumstances will modify the effective priorities, it is likely that the modifications will be subjectively "overlooked" – so that the system of priorities will continue to appear congruent with the "official" model. In the following generations, the discrepancy between the "official" model and effective individual priorities may become increasingly apparent to the individual. Even then, it is likely that the latter will be apprehended and justified in terms that are consistent with the internalized rhetoric of the former. To put it simply: the fathers will, of course, notice the changes in the "objective" conditions of their everyday lives, but neither their systems of "ultimate" significance nor even their effective priorities will be substantially changed. The sons will be more profoundly affected by the changes. Their effective priorities will be modified substantially, while their systems of "ultimate" significance will remain fairly stable. All this on the assumption that not only the fathers but also the sons continue to be socialized *au sérieux* into the "official" model of religion.

This assumption becomes increasingly questionable for later generations. Leaving aside the cumulative effect of continuing social change on everyday life and the growing discrepancy between the system of "ultimate" significance and *effective* priorities, the very character of socialization will be transformed. The *au sérieux* character of the model will be neutralized, to a certain extent, for the grandsons by the fact that they observe the effective priorities governing the lives of the fathers. In simple language: what the fathers preach but do not practice will be internalized by the sons as a system of rhetoric rather than as a system of "ultimate" significance. At the extreme point of such a development – supposing that the "official" model is not adjusted – we find a situation in which everybody is still socialized into the "official" model of religion, but the model is not taken at face value by anybody. Religious practices (such as, service attendance) will be performed for a variety of "nonreligious" motives and specifically religious beliefs will be compartmentalized into opinions (such as, God is almighty) which will have no direct relation to the individuals' effective priorities and everyday conduct.

A further specification of the intermediate types of congruence between the "official" model and individual religiosity must take into account an additional dimension. The exposure of the members of a society to changing "objective" circumstances will vary not only by generation but also by class position, occupation, sex, and so forth. The degree of incongruence between the "official" model and effective priorities will vary accordingly, first in the generation of the fathers and then, in accentuated form, in the generation of the sons, and so forth. If we start out with a situation in which everybody is socialized into the "official" model *au sérieux*, both a "qualitative" and "quantitative" change in this situation will occur in the following generations. At first, almost everybody will continue to be successfully socialized into the "official" model. Only individuals most directly exposed to the "objective" changes will begin to internalize it tongue-in-cheek. Later the major part of the population will still internalize the "official" model, but substantial segments of certain social strata, occupational groups, and so forth will do so tongue-in-cheek. At the same time, the "official" model will have become irrelevant for some individuals whose sons may be no longer socialized into it at all. Still later, only a minority will continue to be socialized into the "official" model *au sérieux*, another segment of the population will internalize it as a system of rhetoric, while the majority of the population will no longer be socialized into it. Eventually, a situation may result in which the typical process of socialization no longer includes the "official" model of religion – more precisely, the former "official" model – and only individuals characterized by social or social-psychological marginality will internalize it as a system of "ultimate" significance. A society in which this is the case is well along the way to a situation in which it is no longer characterized by institutional specialization of religion. We disregard again the possibility that one "official" model is being replaced by another. From the point of view of the dynamics of so-called secularization, this possibility is of subordinate interest.

The general discussion of the consequences of institutional specialization of religion and the formal observations on the relation between the "official" model of religion and individual religiosity prepared the ground for the analysis of religion in modern society. It is apparent that we cannot naïvely attribute the decline of Christianity in its traditional forms to the advance of secularist ideologies, atheism, neopaganism, and the like. The contemporary marginality of church religion and its "inner secularization" appear, rather, as *one* aspect of a complex process in which the long-range consequences of institutional specialization of religion and the global transformations of the social order play a decisive role. What are usually taken as symptoms of the decline of traditional Christianity may be symptoms of a more revolutionary change: the replacement of the institutional specialization of religion by a new social form of religion.

One thing we may assert with confidence: The norms of traditional religious institutions – as congealed in an "official" or formerly "official" model of religion – cannot serve as a yardstick for assessing religion in contemporary society. Before we can arrive at an understanding of religion in modern society, we must, at least, ask the right questions. It was the purpose of our theoretical analysis of the social forms of religion to provide the criteria for deciding what are these questions. What is the hierarchy of significance in the world views of contemporary industrial societies? Is that hierarchy articulated in a sacred cosmos and, if so, how distinct and consistent is this articulation? What are the nature and the origin of the religious representations that constitute the sacred cosmos? What is their basis in the social structure? Are they located in an institutional area that "specializes" in religion? Or are the religious representations distributed over several institutional areas? In other words, can we consider modern religion to be "regressing" to a social form of religion that preceded institutional specialization? Or does the sacred cosmos in modern society have an institutional basis at all? If not, how is the sacred cosmos objectivated in society? – that is, in what way is it part of an objective social reality? What role do the traditional institutions that "specialized" in religion play in this context?

It may be useful, furthermore, to reformulate these questions so as to address them to the corresponding phenomena on the social-psychological level. What are the norms that determine the effective priorities in the everyday lives of typical members of modern industrial societies? What are the subjective relevance systems that have an overarching, sense-integrating function in contemporary life? How clearly are they articulated in individual systems of "ultimate" significance? How are they linked to social roles and positions? To what extent is the traditional "official" model of religion still being internalized and what is its relation to the prevalent systems of "ultimate" significance?

It is one thing to ask questions and another to answer them. With few exceptions, the extensive findings of research in the sociology of religion provide answers only to those questions which directly concern the fate of specialized religious institutions in modern society. Unfortunately, for an assessment of the nature of religion in contemporary society, these are the least important questions. On the other hand, what can one say about the hierarchy of significance in the world views of industrial societies, about the articulation of a sacred cosmos in these world views, about the prevalent individual systems of "ultimate" significance, and so forth? There was no systematic research on these problems. Such research would not only demand a consistent theoretical focus – which we have tried to provide in this essay – but also highly sophisticated methodological procedures. In sum, it is impossible at present to give satisfactory and well-substantiated answers to the questions.

In the absence of such research, two options remain. One consists in a refusal to indulge in speculations and in waiting for the results of future investigations. It would be tempting to choose this option. Considering the significance of the questions for an understanding of modern society, however, the risks involved in opting for the second alternative may be worth taking. The second alternative consists in trying to suggest some answers to the questions on the basis of scattered, limited and, in the main, "weak" evidence. The answers are based on cumulative impressions of the findings of investigations in a variety of areas – such as, industrial and occupational sociology, the family, mass communications, leisure – as well as those few studies in the sociology of religion which go beyond the scope of traditional church religion.

The history of Western civilization is marked by the continuous expansion of institutional specialization of religion. While it is obviously impossible to trace here the many sources of this development, a few summary observations may help to place that development in the context of our present discussion. In the heterogeneous, geographically and socially mobile urban milieu of the Hellenistic world, the sacred cosmos that had become part of that world lost its original, relatively simple relationship to more or less self-contained societies. The partly "disembodied" sacred cosmos was drawn into syncretistic developments which could be accommodated – although with some difficulty – within the framework of the dominant and institutionally nonspecialized religion of the Roman Empire – traditionally rooted in the political and kinship structure of ancient Rome. The eschatological texture of Christian beliefs of the early period and its influence upon the Christian conception of the extent of legitimate political control made such accommodation extremely difficult in the case of Christianity. While submitting to the "properly" defined authority of political institutions, Christianity resisted their traditional *religious* claims. The outcome of the ensuing struggle affected both the character of political institutions in the subsequent history of Europe *and* the direction that was taken by the further development of the incipient church-structure of Christianity. The autonomy of the state was defined in "secular" terms – despite some vestiges of earlier conceptions that survived in the Holy Roman Empire through the feudal period. The autonomy of the church gained a specifically religious significance – despite the "secular" entanglements of religious institutions. The definitions of religious and political jurisdictions were the basis for the variety of arrangements and conflicts between church and state that characterize the subsequent history of Europe.

The church, having remained victorious in a situation of "pluralistic" competition and having adapted herself to the requirements of institutional survival *vis-à-vis* the state, became the visible, specialized institutional basis for *one* well-articulated and obligatory sacred cosmos. Identity between church and religion, and congruence between the "official" model of religion and the prevalent individual systems of "ultimate" significance, was taken for granted in ecclesiastic ideology. For some time, it was also approximated – although not fully accomplished – in fact. We said that the factors that cause a growing incongruence between the "official" model and individual religiosity and disrupt the identity of church and religion are incipiently present in this social form of religion. Until the late Middle Ages, these "seeds of secularization" were here placed in infertile soil. The circumstances which – as we have shown – generally retard the growth of incongruence between the "official" model and individual religiosity prevailed. With the waning of the feudal order, however, the situation began to change. The structural basis for the approximate identity of church and religion was dissolving. The change in the social order transformed the everyday lives and the effective priorities of ever wider strata of the population. The growing discrepancies between the socially prevalent effective priorities and the "official" model undermined the latter and bestowed upon it an increasingly rhetorical status for certain groups in the population – thus permitting, beginning with the Renaissance, the articulation of "secularist" counter-models. In spite of the adjustments of the "official" model of religion during the Reformation and Counter-Reformation, the discrepancies between the "official" model and the socially prevalent effective priorities were not successfully overcome. Church-state relations during the period of absolute monarchies; the political and social context of the "Religious Wars"; the proliferation of sects; the development of scientific thought and its effect on philosophical and – eventually – popular conceptions of life and the universe; the French Revolution and its repercussions in "traditionalist" and "liberal" movements in Catholicism and Protestantism; the social consequences of the Industrial Revolution and the emergence of a working class; and the rise of ideologically oriented political parties, Biblical criticism and its effects on theology, to mention only a few major factors affecting the Christian churches, attest to the danger of oversimplification. Summarizing a complex process, it may be said, nonetheless, that the long-range consequences of institutional specialization of religion as part of an over-all process of social change resulted, paradoxically, in the loss of what institutional specialization originally accomplished in the "pluralistic" religious context of the Hellenistic world and the Roman Empire: monopoly in the definition of an obligatory sacred cosmos.

Political and theological rear-guard actions could retard but did not succeed in preventing eventual legal recognition of a *fait accompli*. "Secular" ideas were competing successfully with the churches in determining the individual systems of "ultimate" significance, especially among those members of the population whose lives and effective priorities had been most radically transformed by "objective" social changes and who were increasingly willing to abandon the traditional "official" model – even as a system of rhetoric. The wealth, power, and administrative perfection of the churches notwithstanding, religion was defined as a private matter. This meant, in practice, that the church could no longer rely on the state to enforce its jurisdictional claims. The church became an institution among other institutions. Its claims and interests were restricted to its "proper" sphere. The "proper" sphere, however, was that of private life. At best, the church was accorded an apparently public status because of its state-supporting "moral" functions. In the period of emerging class-conflict, this turned out to be a hollow privilege.

Institutional specialization of religion, it should be noted, was part of a far-reaching historical process which transformed a traditional social order into modern industrial society. This process was characterized by a complex pattern of successive phases in which political, religious, and economic institutions became increasingly specialized in their functions at the same time that the organization of the institutional areas became increasingly "rational."[18] This process led to the sharp segmentation of the several institutional domains which characterize modern industrial societies. The norms within the separate domains became increasingly "rational" in relation to the *functional* requirements of the institution.[19] The functionally "rational" norms of institutions characterized by a complex division of labor and specialization of roles became increasingly disengaged from the biographical context of meaning in which institutional performances stood for the individual performer. As was indicated earlier, the norms within the separate institutional domains gained a high degree of autonomy. The norms within an institutional domain were thus attached to clearly circumscribed, restricted jurisdictions, but retained unquestioned validity within their jurisdictions.

The church did not escape this development. She gained a high degree of internal autonomy and her institutional structure was characterized by the trend to functional rationality. The validity of her norms became restricted to a specifically "religious sphere," while the global claims of the "official" model were generally neutralized as mere rhetoric. Despite considerable similarity in the development which led to the specialization of economic, political, and religious institutions, however, the process has some peculiar consequences for religion.

Institutional segmentation of the social structure significantly modifies the relation of the individual to the social order as a whole. His "social" existence comes to consist of a series of performances of highly anonymous specialized social roles. In such performances, the person and the personal, biographical context of meaning become irrelevant. At the same time, the "meaning" of performances in one institutional domain, determined by the autonomous norms of that domain, is segregated from the "meaning" of performances in other domains. The "meaning" of such performances is "rational" – but only with respect to the functional requirements of a given institutional area. It is, however, detached from the overarching context of meaning of an individual biography. The missing (or poor) integration of the meaning of institutional performances into a system of *subjective* significance does not disturb the effective functioning of economic and political institutions. As an actor on the social scene, the individual does not liberate himself from the control of institutional norms. Since the "meaning" of these norms only indirectly affects his personal identity and since it has only a "neutral" status in the subjective system of significance, however, the individual does escape the consciousness-shaping effect of institutional norms to a considerable extent. The individual becomes replaceable as a person in proportion to the increasing anonymity of specialized roles that are determined by the functionally rational institutions. More precisely, the subjective biographical context of the performances becomes entirely trivial from the point of view of the institutional domains. The latter need be concerned only with the effective control of performances. The functional rationality of segregated institutional norms tends to make *them* trivial from the point of view of the person who is, therefore, increasingly unlikely to offer subjective resistance to them – a resistance that might be potentially inspired by a conflict between institutional norms and a presumed religious system of significance. The segregation of "rational" institutional norms in the consciousness of the individual is the social-psychological correlate of the institutional segmentation of the social structure.

The segregation of institutionally specialized *religious* norms, however, which originates in the same global processes of social change, seriously affects the function of religious representations. The jurisdiction originally claimed by the "official" model of religion is total, in accordance with the fact that the model is intended to represent a pervasive coherence of sense in the life of the individual. No doubt the global claim of the "official" model of religion can be neutralized, as we have pointed out in the formal analysis of the different modes of internalization of the "official" model. The transformation of specifically religious representations into a system of mere rhetoric, however, necessarily undermines this social form of religion. The approximate congruence between the "official" model of religion and the prevalent subjective systems of "ultimate" significance is lost. We shall have to return to a discussion of some further implications of institutional specialization of religion for the individual in modern society. First, a few remarks on the general consequences of institutional segmentation are in order.

The combination of continued performance control and increasing disengagement from the person which characterizes the primary public institutions in modern industrial societies is the basis for the seeming paradox discussed today under the headings of "individualism" and "conformity." The moral and ideological fervor generated by this discussion tends to preclude an insight into the common structural source of both phenomena. In comparison to traditional social orders, the primary public institutions no longer significantly contribute to the formation of individual consciousness and personality, despite the massive performance control exerted by their functionally rational "mechanisms." Personal identity becomes, essentially, a private phenomenon. This is, perhaps, the most revolutionary trait of modern society. Institutional segmentation left wide areas in the life of the individual unstructured and the overarching biographical context of significance undetermined. From the interstices of the social structure that resulted from institutional segmentation emerged what may be called a "private sphere." The "liberation" of individual consciousness from the social structure and the "freedom" in the "private sphere" provide the basis for the somewhat illusory sense of autonomy which characterizes the typical person in modern society.

We need not discuss here the special problem of the family, beyond a few cursory remarks. The family ceased to be a primary public institution in the sense in which that term applies to political and economic institutions. As the family of procreation" it continues to transmit meanings of overarching biographical significance – more or less successfully. As the "family of orientation" it becomes a basic and, as it were, semi-institutional component of the emerging "private sphere" – a point to which we shall return later. Another problem that cannot be taken up here is the totalitarianism appearing in some modern industrial societies. Its regressive attempts to infuse "public" norms into the "private sphere" and to shape individual consciousness on supra-individual and "irrational" models did not prove successful in the long run.

The sense of autonomy which characterizes the typical individual in modern industrial societies is closely linked to a pervasive consumer orientation. Outside the areas that remain under direct performance control by the primary institutions, the subjective preferences of the individual, only minimally structured by definite norms, determine his conduct. To an immeasurably higher degree than in a traditional social order, the individual is left to his own devices in choosing goods and services, friends, marriage partners, neighbors, hobbies and, as we shall show presently, even "ultimate" meanings in a relatively autonomous fashion.

In a manner of speaking, he is free to construct his own personal identity. The consumer orientation, in short, is not limited to economic products but characterizes the relation of the individual to the entire culture. The latter is no longer an obligatory structure of interpretive and evaluative schemes with a distinct hierarchy of significance. It is, rather, a rich, heterogeneous assortment of possibilities which, in principle, are accessible to any individual consumer. It goes without saying that the consumer preferences still remain a function of the consumer's social biography.

The consumer orientation also pervades the relation of the "autonomous" individual to the sacred cosmos. One highly important consequence of institutional segmentation, in general, and institutional specialization of religion, in particular, is that the specifically religious representations, as congealed in the "official" models of the churches, cease to be the only and obligatory themes in the sacred universe. From the socially determined systems of effective priorities, new themes of "ultimate" significance emerge and, to the extent that they are socially articulated, compete for acceptance in the sacred cosmos. The thematic unity of the traditional sacred cosmos breaks apart. This development reflects the dissolution of *one* hierarchy of significance in the world view. Based on the complex institutional structure and social stratification of industrial societies, different "versions" of the world view emerge. The individual, originally socialized into one of the "versions" may continue to be "loyal" to it, to a certain extent, in later life. Yet, with the pervasiveness of the consumer orientation and the sense of autonomy, the individual is more likely to confront the culture and the sacred cosmos as a "buyer." Once religion is defined as a "private affair," the individual may choose from the assortment of "ultimate" meanings as he sees fit – guided only by the preferences that are determined by his social biography.

An important consequence of this situation is that the individual constructs not only his personal identity but also his individual system of "ultimate" significance. It is true that for such constructions, a variety of models is socially available – but none is "official" in the strict sense of the term (cf. Berger & Luckmann 1966). None is routinely internalized *au sérieux*. Instead, a certain level of subjective reflection and choice determines the formation of individual religiosity – a point that was made earlier (cf. Schelsky 1957). Furthermore, themes of "ultimate" significance emerge primarily out of the "private sphere" and are, on the whole, not yet fully articulated in the culture. The individual systems of "ultimate" significance tend to be, therefore, both syncretistic and vague, in comparison with an "official" model internalized *au sérieux*.

It should be noted that the traditional, specifically religious representations still form part of the heterogeneous sacred cosmos in modern society. They are, indeed, the only part of the sacred cosmos that is commonly recognized as religious. The other elements are usually described as "pseudoreligious" or are not perceived as part of the sacred cosmos, despite the fact that they may be dominant themes in the prevalent individual systems of "ultimate" significance.

The specifically religious representations, furthermore, still form something not unlike a model, a model that bears some resemblance to traditional "official" models of religion. It should be remembered, however, that once the *traditional* sacred cosmos came to reside exclusively in a specialized institution, the jurisdiction of this institution and, indirectly, of the sacred cosmos, was increasingly restricted to the "private sphere." This, in turn, tended to neutralize – although, perhaps, not completely – the privileged status of the traditional "official" model in relation to other themes of "ultimate" significance that addressed themselves to the "inner man." The "autonomous" individual today confronts the traditional specifically religious model more or less as a consumer too. In other words, that model is one of the possible choices of the individual. But even for those who continue to be socialized into the traditional model, specifically religious representations, tend to have a predominantly rhetorical status. Various studies have shown that church-oriented religiosity typically contains only a shallow "doctrinal" layer consisting of "religious opinions" which do not stand in a coherent relation to one another (cf. Pickering 1958: 54–76; cf. Dumont 1958: 77–113; cf. Woelber 1959; cf. Luckmann 1959: 443–446; cf. Schneider & Dornbusch 1958).

The conflict between the claims of the traditional model and the socially determined circumstances of everyday life rarely, if ever, becomes acute – precisely because it is generally taken for granted that these claims are rhetorical. They find no support from other institutions and fail to receive "objective" reaffirmation in the daily lives of the individuals (cf. Tenbruck 1959). The subjective neutralization of these claims, on the other hand, makes it possible for the former "official" model to survive as rhetoric. In the typical case, a conscious rejection of traditional forms of religion, merely because they are not congruent with the effective priorities of everyday life, becomes unnecessary. The neutralization of the claims does, however, contribute to further dissolution of the coherence of the model and reinforces the restriction of specifically religious representations to the "private sphere." The social location of the churches in the contemporary industrial societies decisively influences the selection of those social types who continue to be socialized into the traditional "official" model and determines the manner in which the model is likely to be internalized. Summing up the results of research on church religion, we said that the more "modern" the constellation of factors determining the socialization of the individual, the less likely is the routine internalization of the model and, if internalization still occurs, the less likely will it be *au sérieux*. But even in the case of church-oriented individuals, it is likely that effective priorities of everyday life, the subjective system of "ultimate" significance, and the rhetoric of the traditional "official" model are incongruent – for reasons that were already indicated. An additional reason is the sociability and prestige-substitution function which church religion may continue to perform in the lives of certain types of persons even after the specifically religious function is neutralized.

In view of this situation, it is useful to regard church religiosity in two different perspectives. First, we may view church religiosity as a survival of a traditional social form of religion (that is, institutional specialization) on the periphery of modern industrial societies. Second, we may view church religiosity as one of the many manifestations of an emerging, institutionally nonspecialized social form of religion, the difference being that it still occupies a special place among the other manifestations because of its historical connections to the traditional Christian "official" model. Many phenomena of contemporary church religion make better sense if placed in the second, rather than the first, perspective.

Institutional segmentation of the social structure and the dissolution of the traditional, coherent sacred cosmos affected not only religion as a specialized institution but also the relation of the traditional, specifically religious representations to the values of other specialized institutional domains. The prevalent norms in the various institutional areas, especially economics and politics, were increasingly legitimated by functional rationality. The more autonomous and rational the specialized institutional areas became, the less intimate grew their relation to the transcendent sacred cosmos. The traditional legitimation from "above" (for example, the ethic of vocation and the divine right of kings) is replaced by legitimation from "within" (for example, productivity and independence). In this sense, the norms of the institutional domains did become increasingly "secular." This does not mean, however, that the institutional domains became denuded of "values." "Secularization" in its early phases was not a process in which traditional sacred values simply faded away. It was a process in which autonomous institutional "ideologies" replaced, within their own domain, an overarching and transcendent universe of norms.

This, precisely, constitutes the key problem for the relation of the "modern" individual to the social order. In the long run, isolated institutional "ideologies" were incapable of providing a socially prefabricated *and* subjectively meaningful system of "ultimate" significance. The reasons for this inability, as we have seen, are connected with the social-psychological consequences of institutional segmentation and specialization – with the very processes, in fact, that gave rise to isolated institutional "ideologies." The fate of totalitarianism in modern industrial societies shows that attempts to transform "institutional" ideologies into encompassing world views were not notably successful. Even Communism – which articulated something like an "official" model and which succeeded in enforcing routine socialization of "everybody" into that model in the Soviet Union – seems to have failed in producing a "new man." On the whole, the post-Revolution generations seem to have internalized the "official" model as a system of rhetoric, rather than *au sérieux*. The "retreat into the private sphere," while less conspicous than in "capitalist" countries, is clearly noticeable. The attempts to articulate a coherent and subjectively compelling world view with sacred qualities on the basis of elements taken from "institutional" ideologies (such as "free enterprise"), undertaken in the United States under such pressures as the Cold War and Korea, were doomed to fail because not even tongue-in-cheek internalization could be generally enforced.[20] Furthermore, it proved impossible to create, *ex nihilo* an internal logic that would connect the disparate elements that went into these products.

It was pointed out earlier that the sacred cosmos of modern industrial societies no longer represents *one* obligatory hierarchy and that it is not articulated as a consistent thematic whole. It may sound like an exaggerated metaphor if one speaks of the sacred cosmos of modern industrial societies as *assortments* of "ultimate" meanings. The term points out accurately, however, a significant distinction between the modern sacred cosmos and the sacred cosmos of a traditional social order. The latter contains well-articulated themes which form a universe of "ultimate" significance that is reasonably consistent in terms of its own logic. The former also contains themes that may be legitimately defined as religious; they are capable of being internalized by potential consumers as meanings of "ultimate" significance. These themes, however, do not form a coherent universe. The assortment of religious representations – a sacred *cosmos* in a loose sense of the term only – is not internalized by any potential consumer as a whole. The "autonomous" consumer selects, instead, certain religious themes from the available assortment and builds them into a somewhat precarious private system of "ultimate" significance. Individual religiosity is thus no longer a replica or approximation of an "official" model.

We shall have to return to a discussion of the peculiar character of the sacred cosmos in modern industrial societies. These preliminary observations should suffice, however, to make us aware of the danger of oversimplification in analyzing the social basis of the modern sacred cosmos. The question, properly formulated, is, what are the social bases of the assortment of religious themes prevalent in industrial societies? Our analysis of church religion in modern society sharply pointed up the fact that the modern sacred cosmos as a whole no longer rests on institutions specializing in the maintenance and transmission of a sacred universe. On the basis of our observations on the "secular" institutional ideologies, we may say, furthermore, that the sacred cosmos as a whole does not rest on other primary and specialized institutional areas whose main functions are not religious – as, for example, the state and the economic system. When we turn to a discussion of the origin of various themes in the modern sacred cosmos, we shall have occasion to point out that some themes can be traced back to the traditional Christian cosmos and others to "secular" institutional ideologies. But this is a point that is mainly of historical interest. The effective social basis of the modern sacred cosmos is to be found in neither the churches nor the state nor the economic system.

The social form of religion emerging in modern industrial societies is characterized by the direct accessibility of an assortment of religious representations to potential consumers. The sacred cosmos is mediated neither through a specialized domain of religious institutions nor through other primary public institutions. It is the direct accessibility of the sacred cosmos, more precisely, of an assortment of religious themes, which makes religion today essentially a phenomenon of the "private sphere." The emerging social form of religion thus differs significantly from older social forms of religion which were characterized either by the diffusion of the sacred cosmos through the institutional structure of society or through institutional specialization of religion.

The statement that the sacred cosmos is directly accessible to potential consumers needs to be explicated. It implies that the sacred cosmos is not mediated by primary public institutions and that, correspondingly, no obligatory model of religion is available. It does not imply, of course, that religious themes are not socially mediated in some form. Religious themes originate in experiences in the "private sphere." They rest primarily on emotions and sentiments and are sufficiently unstable to make articulation difficult. They are highly "subjective"; that is, they are not defined in an obligatory fashion by primary institutions. They can be – and are – taken up, however, by what may be called secondary institutions which expressly cater to the "private" needs of "autonomous" consumers. These institutions attempt to articulate the themes arising in the "private sphere" and retransmit the packaged results to potential consumers. Syndicated advice columns, "inspirational" literature ranging from tracts on positive thinking to *Playboy* magazine, *Reader's Digest* versions of popular psychology, the lyrics of popular hits, and so forth, articulate what are, in effect, elements of models of "ultimate" significance. The models are, of course, nonobligatory and must compete on what is, basically, an open market. The manufacture, the packaging and the sale of models of "ultimate" significance are, therefore, determined by consumer preference, and the manufacturer must remain sensitive to the needs and requirements of "autonomous" individuals and their existence in the "private sphere" (cf. Berger & Luckmann 1963).

The appearance of secondary institutions supplying the market for "ultimate" significance does not mean that the sacred cosmos – after a period of institutional specialization – is once again diffused through the social structure. The decisive difference is that the primary public institutions do not maintain the sacred cosmos; they merely regulate the legal and economic frame within which occurs the competition on the "ultimate" significance market. Furthermore, diffusion of the sacred cosmos through the social structure characterizes societies in which the "private sphere," in the strict sense of the term, does not exist and in which the distinction between primary and secondary institutions is meaningless.

The continuous dependence of the secondary institutions on consumer preference and, thus, on the "private sphere" makes it very unlikely that the social objectivation of themes originating in the "private sphere" and catering to it will eventually lead to the articulation of a consistent and closed sacred cosmos and the specialization, once again, of religious institutions. This is one of the several reasons that justify the assumption that we are not merely describing an interregnum between the extinction of one "official" model and the appearance of a new one, but, rather, that we are observing the emergence of a new social form of religion characterized neither by diffusion of the sacred cosmos through the social structure nor by institutional specialization of religion.

The fact that the sacred cosmos rests primarily on the "private sphere" and the secondary institutions catering to the latter, combined with the thematic heterogeneity of the sacred cosmos, has important consequences for the nature of individual religiosity in modern society. In the absence of an "official" model, the individual may select from a variety of themes of "ultimate" significance. The selection is based on consumer preference, which is determined by the social biography of the individual, and similar social biographies will result in similar choices. Given the assortment of religious representations available to potential consumers and given the absence of an "official" model, it is possible, in principle, that the "autonomous" individual will not only select certain themes but will construct with them a well-articulated private *system* of "ultimate" significance. To the extent that some themes in the assortment of "ultimate" meanings are coalesced into something like a coherent model (such as "positive Christianity" and psychoanalysis), some individuals may internalize such models *en bloc*. Unless we postulate a high degree of reflection and conscious deliberation, however, it is more likely that individuals will legitimate the situation-bound (primarily emotional and affective) priorities arising in their "private spheres" by deriving, *ad hoc*, more or less appropriate rhetorical elements from the sacred cosmos. The assumption seems justified, therefore, that the *prevalent* individual systems of "ultimate" significance will consist of a loose and rather unstable hierarchy of "opinions" legitimating the affectively determined priorities of "private" life.

Individual religiosity in modern society receives no massive support and confirmation from the primary public institutions. Overarching subjective structures of meaning are almost completely detached from the functionally rational norms of these institutions. In the absence of external support, subjectively constructed and eclectic systems of "ultimate" significance will have a somewhat precarious reality for the individual (cf. Tenbruck 1959). Also, they will be less stable – or rigid – than the more homogeneous patterns of individual religiosity that characterize societies in which "everybody" internalizes an "official" model and in which the internalized model is socially reinforced throughout an individual's biography. In sum, while the systems of "ultimate" significance in modern society are characterized by considerable variability in content, they are structurally similar. They are *relatively* flexible as well as unstable.

While individual religiosity fails to receive the massive support and confirmation from primary public institutions, it comes to depend upon the more ephemeral support of other "autonomous" individuals. In other words, individual religiosity is socially supported by other persons who, for reasons discussed earlier, are found primarily in the "private sphere." In the "private sphere," the partial sharing, and even joint construction, of systems of "ultimate" significance is possible without conflict with the functionally rational norms of the primary institutions. The so-called nuclear family prevalent in industrial societies performs an important role in providing a structural basis for the "private" production of (rather fleeting) systems of "ultimate" significance. This holds especially for the middle-class family ideal of "partnership marriage" of which it is typically expected that it provide "fulfillment" for the marriage partners (cf. Berger & Kellner 1964: 3–32). If the situation is viewed in this perspective, there is nothing surprising about the upsurge of "familism" in industrial societies, unexpected as this fact would have been for the social scientists of the nineteenth century. On the other hand, the relatively low average stability of the family as an institution becomes readily intelligible if one allows for the extraordinarily heavy social-psychological burden that is placed upon the family by such expectations (cf. Kellner 1966).

Support for subjective systems of "ultimate" significance may also come from persons outside the family. Friends, neighbors, members of cliques formed at work and around hobbies may come to serve as "significant others" who share in the construction and stabilization of "private" universes of "ultimate" significance (cf. Riesman 1950). If such universes coalesce to some degree, the groups supporting them may assume almost sectarian characteristics and develop what we earlier called secondary institutions. This, to list only the most unlikely example, seems to be the case even with such "ultimately" significant hobbies as wife-swapping (cf. Wilson & Meyers 1965). Nevertheless, it is safe to assume that the family remains the most important catalyst of "private" universes of significance.

Notes

16 The increasing autonomy of economic norms and the segregation of specifically economic conduct ("work") in Western history are such well-known facts that they hardly need to be documented by references to a voluminous literature. For a concise discussion of the growing autonomy of political conduct see Plessner 1964.

17 On reflection as a constitutive element of contemporary religiosity, cf. Helmut Schelsky 1957.

18 A large body of literature was devoted to the study of and theories about this process. There is little doubt that the most incisive and seminal discussion of this process is that of Max Weber.

19 The analysis of the general social-psychological implications and consequences of institutional segmentation is based, in the main points, on Gehlen 1949. Reference should be also made to a recent typology of social orders that takes into account, among other things, the degree of institutional specialization in the social structure and articulates its consequences for socialization processes. Cf. Tenbruck, 1962 (1986).

20 Cf. for example, The Report of the President's Commission on National Goals 1950. Cf. also the analysis of the post-Korea "Militant Liberty" Programs of the U.S. Department of Defense, in Janowitz 1960.

VII

MODERN RELIGIOUS THEMES

It was pointed out before that the social basis of the newly emerging religion is to be found in the "private sphere." The themes that have come to occupy a dominant position in the sacred cosmos today originate in and refer to an area of individual existence in modern society that is removed from the primary social institutions. But not all the themes that are available in the sacred cosmos today originate in the "private sphere." Some can be traced back to the traditional Christian cosmos while some others originated in the "secular" institutional ideologies of the eighteenth and nineteenth centuries. Before turning to the discussion of the dominant themes originating in the "private sphere," some remarks on themes with a different origin are therefore in order.

It is apparent that some traditional, *specifically* religious representations survive in the modern sacred cosmos. We are not referring here to the obvious fact that the former "official" Christian model of religion left its imprint upon the world views of all contemporary industrial societies, thereby indirectly influencing the effective priorities in the daily lives of the members of these societies. We refer, rather, to the equally obvious fact that specialized religious institutions continue to be *one* of the sources contributing to the thematic assortment of the modern sacred cosmos. It should be remembered, however, that the character of the religious institutions was radically transformed by the loss of monopoly in defining the sacred cosmos. They no longer transmit, as a matter of course, an obligatory model of religion. They are forced to compete, instead, with many other sources of "ultimate" significance for the attention of "autonomous" individuals who are potential consumers of their "product." Since they alone are recognized as specifically religious and since they can claim a traditional connection to the Christian universe, it may well be that they continue to enjoy a certain advantage in the open market. Despite obvious differences in the public

DOI: 10.4324/9781003257875-8

"image" and, less obviously, the economic basis of, for example, Methodism and *Playboy* magazine, the surviving forms of institutionally specialized religion have taken on the characteristics of what we called secondary institutions. Although the specialized religious institutions have not – entirely – abandoned the traditional Christian rhetoric, that rhetoric increasingly expresses "ultimate" meanings that have only a tenuous relation to the traditional Christian universe (cf. Schneider & Dornbusch 1958).

Some themes that are available in the modern sacred cosmos can be traced to certain values of formerly dominant political and economic ideologies. At present, these themes occupy a subordinate position in the sacred cosmos. Having originated in an underlying context of functional rationality and supra-individual economic and political goals, they cannot be easily converted into elements of "ultimate" subjective significance – for reasons which were discussed at some length before. These ideologies, no matter how "modern" they look, are best understood as late mutations of traditional religion. This view receives some support from the fact that these ideologies were often explicitly formulated as counterreligions and substitute religions. The various attempts to find a source of "ultimate" significance in the specialized economic and political domains do not seem to have had a lasting influence on the modern sacred cosmos. Even in countries where "secular" ideologies with global claims receive the support of the primary public institutions, as in the Soviet Union, they seem to be fighting a losing battle with what is described, locally, as "solipsism," "individualism," and other forms of "bourgeois decadence." It is significant that these phenomena are most conspicuous in the young and urban segments of the population – but are by no means limited to the "hooligans" or "intellectuals." In the United States, the situation differs inasmuch as elements of "secular" ideologies were amalgamated with traditional religious themes and entered the sacred cosmos "in disguise" (cf. Bell 1960).

It should be noted, incidentally, that the traditional religious themes were more easily adapted to the "secular" requirements of the "private sphere" than were the more "transcendent" economic and political values of the "secular" ideologies of the eighteenth and nineteenth centuries. The apparent paradox can be resolved by taking into account the intrinsic "subjective" component of the Christian universe and the stress upon "faith," especially in Protestantism, and by allowing for the differences in the social-psychological context of institutional specialization of religion as against the specialization of the economy and the political domain.

It may be unnecessary to stress again the difficulties in defining and describing the dominant themes in the modern sacred cosmos. The main reasons for these difficulties have already been stated. The religious themes of modern industrial societies do not form a consistently and sharply articulated sacred cosmos. The dominant themes which originate in the "private sphere" are relatively unstable. To the extent that the traditional Christian rhetoric survives, it provides a vocabulary that may hide newly emerging themes. Finally, the themes of "ultimate" significance are internalized in a significantly different manner in different social strata. All this makes a description of the modern sacred cosmos far more difficult than, for example, an exposition of traditional Lutheran dogma. In view of the intrinsic interest and significance of the problem, however, even a tentative sketch of what appear to be the dominant themes in the modern sacred cosmos may be justified.

The dominant themes in the modern sacred cosmos bestow something like a sacred status upon the individual by articulating his "autonomy." This, of course, is consistent with our finding that "ultimate" significance is found by the typical individual in modern industrial societies primarily in the "private sphere" – and thus in his "*private*" biography. The traditional symbolic universes become irrelevant to the everyday experience of the typical individual and lose their character as a (superordinated) reality. The primary social institutions, on the other hand, turn into realities whose sense is alien to the individual. The transcendent social order ceases to be *subjectively* significant both as a representation of an encompassing cosmic meaning and in its concrete institutional manifestations. With respect to matters that "count," the individual is retrenched in the "private sphere." It is of considerable interest that even those subordinate themes in the modern sacred cosmos that are derived from economic and political ideologies tend to be articulated in an increasingly "individualistic" manner – for example, the responsible citizen, the successful business "operator."

The theme of the "autonomous" individual has some historical antecedents, from certain elements in classical Stoicism to the philosophies of the Enlightenment. It received its first modern articulation in the Romantic era. It was then linked to a variety of other themes that ranged from notions of the "freedom of the artist" to nationalism. The theme was rooted socially in the capitalist bourgeoisie and, most conspicuously, in the bohemian fringes of the latter. With the growth and transformation of the middle classes in industrial society, however, the theme became the central topic of the modern sacred cosmos. Even where it was originally linked to a tradition of individual responsibility in a community of individuals (as in the United States), it eventually lost its "transcendent" political halo. The retrenchment of the individual in the "private sphere" – which, as we indicated, presupposes a special, historically unique constellation of social-structural factors – finds a thematic parallel in the redefinition of personal identity to mean the "inner man." Individual "autonomy" thus comes to stand for absence of external restraints and traditional taboos in the private search for identity.

The theme of individual "autonomy" found many different expressions. Since the "inner man" is, in effect, an undefinable entity, its presumed discovery involves a lifelong quest. The individual who is to find a source of "ultimate" significance in the subjective dimension of his biography embarks upon a process of self-realization and self-expression that is, perhaps, not continuous – since it is immersed in the recurrent routines of everyday life – but certainly interminable. In the modern sacred cosmos, self-expression and self-realization represent the most important expressions of the ruling topic of individual "autonomy." Because the individual's performances are controlled by the primary public institutions, he soon recognizes the limits of his "autonomy" and learns to confine the quest for self-realization to the "private sphere." The young may experience some difficulty in accepting this restriction – a restriction whose "logic" is hardly obvious until one learns to appreciate the "hard facts of life." Content analysis of popular literature, radio and television, advice columns, and inspirational books provides ample evidence that self-expression and self-realization are prominent themes indeed. They also occupy a central position in the philosophy, if not always the practice, of education. The individual's natural difficulty in discovering his "inner Self" explains, furthermore, the tremendous success of various scientific and quasi-scientific psychologies in supplying guidelines for his search (cf. Berger 1965).

The prevalent mobility ethos can be considered a specific expression of the theme of self-realization.[21] Self-realization by means of status achievement precludes, of course, a radical retrenchment in the "private sphere." It is significant, however, that the mobility ethos is typically linked to an attitude toward the social order which is both "individualistic" and manipulative. Finally, since there is a structurally determined discrepancy between the mobility ethos and status achievement, the hypothesis may be put forth that the "failures" will have a reinforced motivation for retrenchment in the "private sphere" (Luckmann & Berger 1964).

Another, peculiarly modern, articulation of the themes of self-expression and self-realization is sexuality. In view of the prominent place occupied by sexuality in the modern sacred cosmos, however, it deserves special consideration. The rigidity with which various aspects of sexual conduct are institutionalized in traditional societies attests to the difficulty in regulating such basic and, in a sense, "private" conduct by external controls – as well as to the importance of such regulation for the kinship system. Wherever the kinship system is a central dimension of the social structure, pertinent norms are typically endowed with religious significance and are socially enforced. With specialization of the primary institutional domains, however, the family and, thus, sexuality lose some of their relevance for those domains and the enforcement of norms regulating the family and sexual conduct *becomes less important.* One may say, with some qualifications, that the family and sexuality recede more and more into the "private sphere." Conversely, to the extent that sexuality is "freed" from external social control, it becomes capable of assuming a crucial function in the "autonomous" individual's quest for self-expression and self-realization. This argument obviously does not imply that sexuality was unimportant or lacked urgency for men before the modern industrial period. Nor does it imply that sexuality did not have religious significance in the traditional sacred cosmos. It does imply, however, that sexuality, in connection with the "sacred" themes of self-expression and self-realization, now comes to play a unique role as a source of "ultimate" significance for the individual who is retrenched in the "private sphere." It is likely that the development which led from the notions of romantic love to what we may call, tongue-in-cheek, the sexual polytheism of the respectable suburbanite, represents more than a shortlived swing of the pendulum from which the weights of Victorian taboos were removed.

The far-reaching (although, of course, not complete) "liberation" of sexuality from social control permits sexual conduct to be governed more radically than in a traditional social order by consumer preference. It should be noted, however, that sexuality – while a basic component of individual "autonomy" – permits an enlargement of the "private sphere" beyond the solitary individual and, thus, may serve as a form of self-transcendence. At the same time, it is a form of self-transcendence which remains limited to the "private sphere" and is, one is tempted to say, innocuous from the point of view of a social order that is based, essentially, upon the functionally rational norms of the primary public institutions.

Another theme which occupies an important place in the sacred cosmos of modern industrial societies is familism. This may appear surprising, at first, because it is obvious that the family lost many functions which it traditionally performed in the social structure. Resuming the argument put forth in the discussion of sexuality, however, we may say that it was precisely the loss of these functions which made the family recede into the "private sphere" and which enabled it to become a source of "ultimate" significance for the individual retrenched in the "private sphere." Familism as a theme in the modern sacred cosmos bears a superficial resemblance only to the place occupied by the family in traditional religious universes – such as the kinship-centered values of traditional Chinese society. In the latter, the family as well as the state were elements in – and representations of – a cosmic order. Modern familism, on the other hand, represents an expansion of the "private sphere" beyond the confines of the solitary individual – an expansion that again, just as self-transcendence in sexuality, does not conflict with the norms and the functional requirements of the primary public institutions. Self-transcendence in the family differs from that in sexuality insofar as it is, potentially at least, more stable – permitting the construction of a microcosm that may be of "ultimate" significance throughout a biography.

It is apparent that the theme of familism is closely linked to the theme of sexuality. In the modern sacred cosmos, the two are becoming increasingly compatible. The consumer-orientation of the "autonomous" individual allows for the inclusion of both themes in a subjective system of relevance. It should be noted, however, that the "this world" nature of modern familism is more successfully camouflaged by a vocabulary derived from the traditional Christian rhetoric than that of sexuality or, for that matter, of any other dominant "sacred" theme. It is the one modern theme which can be supported by the surviving forms of institutionally specialized religion with the least contradiction in their "internal logic."

The major themes of individual "autonomy," self-expression, self-realization, the mobility ethos, sexuality, and familism are surrounded by a host of less important topics which, nonetheless, have some claim to "sacred" status. The latter are, of course, equally available for the "autonomous" individual in the assortment of religious representations. They are subordinated to the major themes in the sense that they are less likely to be selected as cornerstones in the construction of subjective systems of "ultimate" significance. As pointed out earlier, many of the subordinate themes originate either in the traditional Christian cosmos or in the "secular" ideologies of the eighteenth and nineteenth centuries. It is impossible to try to offer even a tentative sketch of these subordinate themes here. For the sake of illustration, we shall mention only those topics which emerged from the peculiarly American dialectics of the egalitarian democratic tradition and the mobility ethos: "getting along with others," "adjustment," "a fair shake for all," "togetherness." It must be admitted that it is extremely difficult to assess the importance of these themes. It is at least conceivable that they are often merely part of a rhetoric whose function it is to make the dominant theme of individual "autonomy" more acceptable – especially in its least "private" expression as an "ethos" of social mobility.

It is interesting to note that death does not appear even as a subordinate topic in the sacred cosmos of a modern industrial society. Nor are growing old and old age endowed with "sacred" significance. The "autonomous" individual is young and he never dies.[22]

It may be said, in sum, that the modern sacred cosmos symbolizes the social-historical phenomenon of individualism and that it bestows, in various articulations, "ultimate" significance upon the structurally determined phenomenon of the "private sphere." We tried to show that the structure of the modern sacred cosmos and its thematic content represent the emergence of a new social form of religion which, in turn, is determined by a radical transformation in the relation of the individual to the social order.

Notes

21 For the classical discussion of the mobility ethos and its social-psychological implications cf. Merton 1957, pp. 131–194.

22 For an excellent theoretical probe into the causes of the adolescent traits to be found in contemporary culture cf. Friedrich Tenbruck 1961.

POSTSCRIPT

In the definition of the problem and in the description of the character of religion in modern society, we adopted and tried to maintain an attitude of detachment. We hoped to avoid thereby the narrowing of perspectives that results so frequently in the analysis of religion not only from the various distinct forms of ideological bias but also from assumptions that are commonly taken for granted even in sociological theory. Where the analysis was supported directly by empirical evidence, it was necessary merely to exercise a certain amount of caution in generalizing from the data. Where the argumentation had to rely on indirect and scattered evidence, however, it was clearly impossible to refrain from using criteria of relevance which were derived from the implications of a theoretical position. In this case, the temptation to overinterpret symptoms and to see connections which are merely plausible is indubitably great and we stress again the tentative character of some of the conclusions that were advanced. Nevertheless, we tried throughout to hold ourselves to the task at hand, to analyze rather than to evaluate. The question of how the profound changes in the character of religion in modern society affect individual existence, however, touches upon matters of personal concern to everyone. It may be permissible, at the end, to relax the neutrality to which we felt obligated during the previous discussion.

The discrepancy between the subjective "autonomy" of the individual in modern society and the objective autonomy of the primary institutional domains strikes us as critical. The primary social institutions have "emigrated" from the sacred cosmos. Their functional rationality is not part of a system that could be of "ultimate" significance to the individuals in the society. This removes from the primary institutions much of the (potentially intolerant) human pathos that proved to be fateful all too often in human history. If the process could be viewed in isolation, it could justifiably appear as an essential component in freeing social arrangements from primitive emotions. The increasing autonomy of the primary public institutions, however, has consequences for the relation of the individual to the social order – and thus, ultimately, to himself. Reviewing some of these consequences, one is equally justified in describing this process as a process of dehumanization of the basic structural components of the social order. The functional rationality of the primary social institutions seems to reinforce the isolation of the individual from his society, contributing thereby to the precariousness inherent in all social orders. Autonomy of the primary institutions, "subjective" autonomy and *anomie* of the social order are dialectically related. At the very least, it may be said that "subjective" autonomy and autonomy of the primary institutions, the two most remarkable characteristics of modern industrial societies, are genuinely ambivalent phenomena.

The new social form of religion emerges in the same global transformation of society which leads to the autonomy of the primary public institutions. The modern sacred cosmos legitimates the retreat of the individual into the "private sphere" and sanctifies his subjective "autonomy." Thus it inevitably reinforces the autonomous functioning of the primary institutions. By bestowing a sacred quality upon the increasing subjectivity of human existence, it supports not only the secularization but also what we called the dehumanization of the social structure. If this still appears paradoxical, we have failed in driving home the point of this essay.

The modern sacred cosmos appears to operate as a *total* ideology. It provides an encompassing assortment of plausible ideas which supports the functioning of modern industrial societies – but *without* explicitly legitimating them. The final clause in the preceding sentence indicates one reason why it is not particularly useful to call the new social form of religion an ideology in the ordinary sense. In addition, the new social form of religion does *not* represent the vested interests of a particular social stratum and it is not articulated as a program of political and social action. It is neither utopian nor restorationist, neither communist nor capitalistic. It is doubtful whether the traditional social forms of religion can be adequately understood by attaching to them the label of ideology, notwithstanding their occasional ideological functions. The label would be indubitably misplaced in the case of the new social form of religion – for the reasons that were just mentioned.

How is one to decide whether the new social form of religion is "good" or "bad"? It is a radically subjective form of "religiosity" that is characterized by a weakly coherent and nonobligatory sacred cosmos and by a low degree of "transcendence" in comparison to traditional modes of religion. Is this good or bad?

While the new social form of religion supports the dehumanization of the social structure, it also "sacralizes" the (relative) liberation of human *consciousness* from the constraint of the latter. This liberation represents a historically unprecedented opportunity for the autonomy of personal life for "everybody." It also contains a serious danger – of motivating mass withdrawal into the "private sphere" while "Rome burns." On balance, is this good or bad?

No matter how one answers this question, the effort to try to understand what is a revolutionary change in the relation of the individual to the social order can hardly be misspent. The emergence of the new social form of religion is partly obscured by the more easily visible economic and political characteristics of modern industrial society. It is unlikely that the trend we have tried to describe is reversible – even if such a reversal were considered desirable. One must not avoid seeing it because one clings to traditionalist religious illusions. Nor must one ignore its implications because one may be inspired by secularist optimism.

REFERENCES

Chapter I

Luckmann, T. (1960). Neuere Schriften zur Religionssoziologie. *Kölner Zeitschrift für Soziologie und Sozialpsychologie* 12(2), pp. 315–326.

Parsons, T. (1949). *Essays in Sociological Theory Pure and Applied*. New York: The Free Press.

Chapter II

Berger, P. (1961). *The Noise of Solemn Assemblies: Christian Commitment and the Religious Establishment in America*. Garden City: Doubleday.

Bras, G. L. (1960). Problèmes de la Sociologie des Religions. In G. Gurvitch, *Traité de la Sociologie, Vol. II*. (pp. 79–102). Paris: Presses Universitaires de France.

Fichter, J. H. (1951). *Dynamics of a City Church: Southern Parish, Vol. I*. Chicago: The University of Chicago Press.

Fichter, J. H. (1954). *Social Relations in the Urban Parish*. Chicago: The University of Chicago Press.

Glock, C. Y. (1959). The Sociology of Religion. In R. K. Merton, L. Broom, & L. S. Cottrell Jr., *Sociology Today: Problems and Prospects* (pp. 153–177). New York: Basic Books.

Goldschmidt, D., Greiner, F., & Schelsky, H. (1959). *Soziologie der Kirchengemeinde*. Stuttgart: Enke.

Goldschmidt, D., & Matthes, J. (1962). Probleme der Religionssoziologie. *Kölner Zeitschrift für Soziologie und Sozialpsychologie*, Special Issue No. 6.

Herberg, W. (1955). *Protestant, Catholic and Jew: An Essay in American Religious Sociology*. Garden City: Doubleday.

Honigsheim, P. (1957). Sociology of Religion: Complementary Analyses of Religious Institutions. In H. Becker & A. Boskoff, *Modern Sociological Theory in Continuity and Change* (pp. 450–481). New York: The Dryden Press.

Hunt, C. L. (1958). The Sociology of Religion. In J. S. Roucek, *Contemporary Sociology*. New York: Philosophical Library.
Koester, R. (1959). *Die Kirchentreuen*. Stuttgart: Enke.
Lambert, R. D. (1960). *The Annals of the American Society of Political and Social Science, Vol. 332: Religion in American Society*. Philadelphia: Sage.
Lenski, G. (1961). *The Religious Factor: A Sociological Study of Religion's Impact on Politics, Economics and Family Life*. Garden City: Doubleday.
Schneider, L., & Dornbusch, S. M. (1958). *Popular Religion: Inspirational Books in America*. Chicago: The University of Chicago Press.
Tenbruck, F. (1959). Die Kirchengemeinde in der entkirchlichten Gesellschaft: Ergebnisse und Deutung der "Reultingen-Studie". In D. Goldschmidt, F. Greiner, & H. Schelsky, *Soziologie der Kirchengemeinde* (pp. 122–132). Stuttgart: Enke.

Chapter III

Berger, P., & Luckmann, T. (1966). *The Social Construction of Reality: A Treatise of the Sociology of Knowledge*. Garden City: Doubleday.
Cooley, C. H. (1909). *Social Organization: A Study of the Larger Mind*. New York: Scribner's.
Cooley, C. H. (1922). *Human Nature and the Social Order*. Revised ed. New York: Sribner's.
Halbwachs, M. (1925). *Les Cadres Sociaux de la Mémoire*. Paris: Presses Universitaires de France.
Halbwachs, M. (1950). *La Mémoire Collective*. Paris: Presses Universitaires de France.
Mead, G. H. (1934). *Mind, Self & Society from the Standpoint of a Social Behaviorist*. Chicago: The University of Chicago Press.
Sartre, J.-P. (1957). *The Transcendence of the Ego: An Existentialist Theory of Consciousness*. New York: The Noonday Press.
Schutz, A. (1962). On Multiple Realities; Symbol, Reality and Society. In A. Schutz, *Collected Papers, Vol I* (pp. 207–259, 287–356). The Hague: Martinus Nijhoff.
Schutz, A. (1964). *Collected Papers, Vol. II*. The Hague: Martinus Nijhoff.
Washburn, S. L. (1962). *Social Life of Early Man*. London: Methuen.

Chapter IV

Berger, P., & Luckmann, T. (1966). *The Social Construction of Reality: A Treatise in the Sociology of Knowledge*. Garden City: Doubleday.
Hoijer, H. (1954). *Language in Culture: Conference on the Interrelations of Language and Other Aspects of Culture*. Chicago: The University of Chicago Press.
Luckmann, T. (1969). Die Soziologie der Sprache. In R. König, *Handbuch der empirischen Sozialforschung, Vol. II* (pp. 1050–1101). Stuttgart: Enke.
Snell, B. (1955). *Die Entdeckung des Geistes: Studien zur Entstehung des europäischen Denkens bei den Griechen*. Hamburg: Claasen.
Swanson, G. E. (1960). *The Birth of the Gods: The Origin of Primitive Beliefs*. Ann Arbor: The University of Michigan Press.
Voegelin, E. (1952). *The New Science of Politics: An Introduction*. Chicago: The University of Chicago Press.

von Humboldt, W. (1953). Über die Verschiedenheit des menschlichen Sprachbaues und ihren Einfluss auf die geistige Entwicklung des Menschengeschlechts. In W. von Humboldt, *Werke, Vol. III* (pp. 463–473). Darmstadt: Wissenschaftliche Buchgesellschaft.

Wach, J. (1944). *Sociology of Religion*. Chicago: The University of Chicago Press.

Webster, T. (Session 1952–1953). Language and Thought in Early Greece. *Memoirs and Proceedings of the Manchester Literary and Philosophical Society*, pp. 1–22.

Whorf, B. L. (1956). Languages and Logic. In B. L. Whorf, *Language, Thought and Reality* (pp. 233–245). Cambridge: The Technology Press of Massachusetts Institute of Technology.

Chapter V

Fichter, J. H. (1951). *Dynamics of a City Church: Southern Parish, Vol. I.* Chicago: The University of Chicago Press.

Fichter, J. H. (1954). *Social Relations in the Urban Parish*. Chicago: The University of Chicago Press.

Luckmann, T. (1959a). Four Protestant Parishes in Germany. *Social Research* 26, pp. 423–448.

Luckmann, T. (1959b). Vier protestantische Kirchengemeinden. In D. Goldschmidt, F. Greiner, & H. Schelsky, *Soziologie der Kirchengemeinde* (pp. 132–144). Stuttgart: Enke.

Chapter VI

Berger, P., & Kellner, H. (1964). Marriage and the Construction of Reality. *Diogène* 46(2), pp. 3–32.

Berger, P., & Luckmann, T. (1963). Sociology of Religion and Sociology of Knowledge. *Sociology and Social Research* 47(4), pp. 417–427.

Berger, P., & Luckmann, T. (1966). Secularization and Pluralism. *International Yearbook for the Sociology of Religion* 2, pp. 73–86.

Dumont, J. (1958). Sondage sur la Mentalité Religieuse d'Ouvriers en Wallonie. In E. a. Collard, *Vocation de la Sociologie Religieuse; Sociologie des Vocations* (pp. 77–113). Tournai: Casterman.

Gehlen, A. (1949). *Die Seele im technischen Zeitalter: Sozialpsychologische Probleme der industriellen Gesellschaft*. Tübingen: Mohr (Siebeck).

Janowitz, M. (1960). *The Professional Soldier*. New York: The Free Press.

Kellner, H. (1966). *Dimensions of the Individual's Conception of Social Reality Arising Within Marriage*. Unpublished Ph.D., Graduate Faculty, New School for Social Research.

Luckmann, T. (1959). Four Protestant Parishes in Germany. *Social Research* 26(4), pp. 423–448.

Pickering, W. (1958). Quelques Résultats d'Interviews Religieuses. In E. a. Collard, *Vocation de la Sociologie Religieuse; Sociologie des Vocations* (pp. 54–76). Tournai: Casterman.

Plessner, H. (1964). The Emancipation of Power. *Social Research* 31(2), pp. 155–174.

President's Commission on National Goals, A. A. (1960). *Goals for Americans: Comprising The Report of the President's Commission on National Goals and Chapters Submitted for the Consideration of the Commission*. Englewood Cliffs, NJ: Prentice-Hall.

Riesman, D. (1950). *The Lonely Crowd*. New Haven: Yale University Press.

Schelsky, H. (1957). Ist die Dauerreflektion institutionalisierbar? – Zum Thema einer modernen Religionssoziologie. *Zeitschrift für Evangelische Ethik* 1(4), pp. 153–174.

Schneider, L., & Dornbusch, S. M. (1958). *Popular Religion: Inspirational Books in America.* Chicago: The University of Chicago Press.

Tenbruck, F. (1959). Die Kirchengemeinde in der entkirchlichten Gesellschaft: Ergebnisse und Deutung der "Reutlingen-Studie". In D. Goldschmidt, F. Greiner, & H. Schelsky, *Soziologie der Kirchengemeinde* (pp. 122–132). Stuttgart: Enke.

Tenbruck, F. (1962). *Geschichte und Gesellschaft.* University of Freiburg, Habilitationsschrift. published 1986, Berlin: Duncker & Humblot.

Wilson, T. J., & Meyers, E. (1965). *Wife Swapping; A Complete Eight Year Survey of Morals in America.* New York: Counterpoint.

Woelber, H. O. (1959). *Religion ohne Entscheidung; Volkskirche am Beispiel der jungen Generation.* Göttingen: Vandenhoeck & Ruprecht.

Chapter VII

Bell, D. (1960). *The End of Ideology.* New York: The Free Press.

Berger, P. (1965). Towards a Sociological Understanding of Psychoanalysis. *Social Research* 32(1), pp. 26–41.

Luckmann, T., & Berger, P. (1964). Social Mobility and Personal Identity. *European Journal of Sociology* 5(2), pp. 331–344.

Merton, R. (1957). *Social Theory and Social Structure.* Revised ed. New York: The Free Press.

Schneider, L., & Dornbusch, S. M. (1958). *Popular Religion: Inspirational Books in America.* Chicago: The University of Chicago Press.

Tenbruck, F. (1961). La Jeunesse Moderne. *Diogène* 36, pp. 3–36.

SUPPLEMENT TO THE 1991 GERMAN EDITION[1]

Editors' Comment

Luckmann added the following postscript to the German re-translation of The Invisible Religion, *published in 1991 by Suhrkamp. That edition was encouraged and inspired by Hubert Knoblauch, who provided a highly accessible German version that corresponded to sociology of religion's revival in the 1990s in German speaking sociology. In addition, Knoblauch's retranslation of the text provided a fresh terminology, sensitive to capturing the unestablished forms of religion outside of churches. It was his great contribution that he was able to contextualize Luckmann's approach within sociology of religion's larger history in the development of the discipline, emphasizing the fundamental role of the social construction of meaning with a far broader scope than the narrow perspective typical of church sociology. Empirically, Luckmann's assertions, dating from the 1960s, turned out to be highly valuable to understanding the shift in the widespread religious practices of our contemporaries. This development became socially highly visible during the 1990s, and has continued to accompany the ongoing transformation of religion in the following decades. Luckmann anticipated the emergence of a completely new social form of religion. There is still ongoing debate about Luckmann's theoretical idea that he proposed purposely to criticize secularization theory. The main objection targets Luckmann's broad anthropological definition of religion. In the following addendum, he counters this criticism without abandoning his main tenets. The text shows an important development in Luckmann's sociological theory of religion. It helps correct the most frequently repeated, yet inaccurate, classification that subsumes Luckmann's sociology of religion as purely "functionalist," compared to the seemingly more "substantial" version developed by his colleague and coauthor Peter L. Berger.*

In this addendum, Luckmann introduces aspects one could be inclined to interpret as religious in substance. *In this text, there is a clear modification concerning his understanding of religion, regardless of his repeated claims of sticking to his theory from the beginning of his writing on religion. Here, the "social" perspective – i.e., the* functional *role of providing the brute fabric of social structure with meaning, more precisely, by establishing a system of ultimate meaning – is complemented by notions regarding the* experiential *dimension of religion, the "subjective" perspective. Drawing on Schutz's ideas regarding the processes of transcending the* hic et nunc *within the stream of consciousness, Luckmann develops a sociological approach to religious experience. The following text is crucial for a more thorough understanding of Luckmann's sociology of religion. Therefore, we are pleased to add this chapter to the present English reissue of* The Invisible Religion. *Re-translating an author into one of the languages he has admirably dominated is almost an impossible task. Any shortcomings should be attributed not to Luckmann, but to our translation efforts.*

I. Introduction

Today when writing this, approximately a quarter century after the book's first publication in 1965, there is still the widespread view of modernity as "bereft of any religion," and as essentially areligious. I continue to consider this view to be principally wrong. If it applies to anything at all, it does not characterize Modernity in general, but rather concerns social structure in the narrowest sense of the term. Compared with the societies of Australian aborigines, ancient Egypt, and the European Middle Ages, industrial societies may indeed appear secular and rationalistic. Their formative political and religious institutions have ceased to depend on traditional, specifically religious, legitimations. Their prevailing cosmology, provided by modern science, no longer invoke *apparently* religious myths, and their dominant ideologies rely on science as the rhetorical original primary source of their legitimations. Most people living in modern industrial societies no longer obey, strictly and exclusively, one particular, officially established religious tradition, including all its mandatory dogmas and rites. Hence, the social structures of the modern world are "secular" to an extent unknown in earlier times and other societies.

But as much as people in modern societies may differ in their lifestyle from other cultures, the basic religious condition of their life has not been lost. It has always characterized the human condition, probably in distinction to other species' ways of life. All fundamental social and cultural transformations have done nothing to alter the essentially religious nature of the human condition. The social circumstances of modern life did not create an entirely novel human nature. The main themes of socially constructed models of reality have undoubtedly changed. And because of the structural changes which led to modern society, the typical patterns to which the individual's consciousness is oriented have also changed. However, the modeling itself, which places the individual in a socially and historically transcendent reality, is a religious process. The process of inserting an individual organism of the species *homo sapiens* into the transcendence of a historical society is religious, even if experiences of greater transcendence are not preconstructed in this society or, if they are, some – or many – individuals do not orient themselves toward these preconstructed models.

Obviously, my assertion rests upon a particular view of "religion" and "transcendence." Since writing the book, my view has not changed substantially. However, I have broadened and specified it regarding the concept of the experience of transcendence. It is still my view that the basic function of "religion" is to transform members of the natural species into actors in a historical social order. Religion exists wherever the conduct of member of a species turns into morally accountable actions; where a Self finds itself in a world inhabited by other beings with whom, for whom, and against whom it acts in a morally accountable way.

Today, it still requires effort to free ourselves from the ethnocentric assumption that religion is only that which conforms to the experience of religion in our own society. However, when looking at the history of human conduct and suffering, we observe an overwhelming variety of social orders serving the basic religious function of embedding human beings in the historical social order. The totemism of the Arunta, the tribal cultures of the Sioux and the Vikings, Siberian Shamanism, the divine cosmos of the Egyptians, the Yahwism of Ancient Israel, the different Hindu and Buddhist forms of religion, Confucianism, the Greek Olympus, the old Roman state religion, Christianity, varying from syncretistic Sicilian popular Catholicism to the Puritan communities of New England, Haitian Voodoo culture, American civil religion, and Sōka Gakkai in Japan all seem to have very little in common. In fact, the "contents" of these social orders and their religions differ enormously. This is because these vastly divergent contents are produced by two closely linked social processes in which ordinary human reality is linked, more or less systematically, to something that is taken to transcend it, to "another" reality. Both processes are communicative, although on different levels of complexity, and regarding diverse social-structural embeddings.

In the first process, subjective experience of several this-worldly or otherworldly transcendences is articulated by using signs (verbally, symbolically) and reconstructed (usually for others, that is, intersubjectively). It is on these reconstructions that subsequent processes of social communication elaborate, in the course of which some reconstructions are discarded, while others are consolidated. Related to each other systematically, they serve as testimony to "another" reality what enables the collective ontologizing of the subjective experience of transcendence. Some remarks on this later. But first, we need to clarify what is referred to by "transcendence" and subjective experience of transcendence, and with the concept of "another" reality.

II. Experiences of Transcendence

Without going into detail, one can say that everyone is aware of the transcendence of the world in which he or she lives. This horizon of consciousness is based on the fact that everyday life experience hits boundaries. One may transcend them within this reality, or by leaping to another reality, or one may be stopped by them. Everyone knows about the limits *within* the world, and also knows that the world as I experience it has boundaries. Nobody seriously doubts that the world into which she or he was born existed long before he or she became aware of its existence, and nobody expects the world to end when his or her consciousness of it ends. Furthermore, in our "naturally" pragmatic everyday life-attitude, we take it for granted that many things happen we do not want to happen, and that many things do not occur we want to occur. Frequently, we must wait – and often we wait in vain. Many things we worked toward full of hope dwindle away. On the other hand, our actions leave traces, even unwantedly, which we encounter long after we have forgotten the action. Every human being discovers that he or she is not alone in the world. We meet other beings who are remarkably like ourselves. We see that others grow older and die. We know that they themselves were born, and we conclude that others will survive us. We routinely wake up each day and fall asleep at night. We get used to certain procedures; we adopt long-established orders. Everyday life takes its familiar course. Its limits do not frighten us very much. But what if we lose old habits, and the prospect of not waking up dismays us?

In everyday life, we all experience the world as a reality we belong to, but with which we are not identical. Although we can familiarize with it, we cannot become united with it. Prereflexively, everyone can easily distinguish between self-related and self-transcending experience. It is deeply engrained in our subjective knowledge that the world transcends us. This distinction is rooted in the general structure of our experience. Not even the simplest perceptual experience is enclosed in itself: it contains some of the immediate past, it anticipates some of the immediate future. The inner core of any actual experience is surrounded by a horizon of that which is currently not experienced: the experiential core automatically points – prospectively – to what has not yet been experienced and – retrospectively – to what is no longer experienced. Consequently, the primordial "co-experience" of transcendence is an integral part of our mundane experience of everyday life. It is the distinction between self-related and self-transcendent experience, along with that primordial "co-experience" of transcendence that forms the basis for the stratification of our lifeworld experience into everyday reality with its limits, the boundaries of the mundane including its transcendence by the extraordinary, and the confines beyond what can be experienced at all.

Thus, we can formulate a simplified typology of experiences of "transcendence." First, whenever anything transcends that which at the moment is concretely given in actual, direct experience, and can itself be experienced in the same manner as that which it now transcends, we may speak of "little" transcendences of everyday life. Second, when that which is actually experienced is taken to refer to something that cannot be experienced directly, one may speak of the "intermediate" transcendences of everyday life, *provided* that that which cannot be, itself, experienced directly is taken to belong to the same *everyday* reality as the

Self. Third, when an experience presents itself as pointing to something that not only cannot be experienced directly but, in addition, is definitively not part of an ordinary reality in which things can be seen, touched, handled, one may speak of the "great" transcendences.

Yet the instances of "little" transcendences are not at all purely trivial matters. However, we usually take it for granted that we can transcend them, because they are only linked to the spatial and temporal limits of our experience in this moment and our current action. Essentially, there is nothing that impedes us from bypassing or transcending them in future experience and subsequent actions. However, even dealing with the "little" transcendences of space and time is a considerable achievement. Usually, we realize this only when our movement is impaired, when we become forgetful, or when we wait in vain. For humans, "coping" with these kinds of transcendences always remains provisional: After we have crossed one of these boundaries, we arrive at the next. After one wait is done, the subsequent one starts, et cetera.

Within our surroundings, we meet bodies which are not objects, but are perceived as persons like us, who are located as Selves in their world of actual reach which, conversely, includes ourselves. Our world of actual reach may overlap significantly with that of the others. It can, though, never be completely identical, as our fellow human beings have their own spatiotemporal and biographical perspectives, and I have my own. However, we usually disregard these details. In our experience of others, we encounter the boundaries of our own experience and, simultaneously, meet the limits of our experience of the other. The boundary one encounters when experiencing instances of "intermediate" transcendences cannot be crossed, however permeable it may occasionally appear, e.g., in the ecstasy of great love. The other's "outward" represents an "inward" that cannot be sensed as such directly. But it represents it so intimately that we may get the impression that the inward can be accessed directly through the outward. In cases of "little" and "intermediate" transcendences, the boundaries of experience are drawn in one and the same province of reality, and can be crossed in a prosaic, almost habitual, process by directing or withdrawing our attention of consciousness.

Things are somewhat different in the withdrawal from everyday life that characterizes sleep and dreams. Here, subjective experience, and even consciousness itself, are facing a boundary different from its own inevitable end, a different fringe than that of the respective world of actual reach, a different barrier than that which separates one human from the other. The cessation of our usual performances of consciousness brings us to a boundary behind which something lies that is completely different from what is before it. We experience another reality than that of everyday life. What is noteworthy about this reality is that we enter it daily or nightly by crossing a line of experience beyond which there is no analogous experience, and from which we return by crossing an equally distinctly marked boundary. In contrast to boundary crossings within everyday life reality, there is little we can take with us, and little that we can bring back. Between the complete departure from everyday life during sleep, and the lowest level of habitual everyday attention, there lies an area of tension of consciousness of being half awake, where the differences are only faintly graded. Likewise, the ecstatic transitions do not have to be performed in one big leap. The states of being half awake and of being in ecstasy share with dreams the uncommon feature that the relevance structures that dominate everyday life are largely or completely suspended. Everyday concerns fade away. In all these boundary crossings, everyday life loses its reality accent in favor of another state. What these experiences point to may be inferred subjectively. Given at least some basic scheme of socially convincing preconstructed interpretations, such experiences may lose their transitory character, and attain some permanent claim to reality that maintains its *preeminence* even after "returning" to everyday life. The natural attitude is discarded, the pragmatic motive is suspended, the relevance systems of everyday action and everyday experience are largely disabled. For everyday practice, however, this is only limitedly effective, even if the socially constructed and canonized worldview marks everyday life, and *not* the other reality, as ephemeral illusion.

Death is a different issue. One's own death cannot be experienced as a boundary. Rather, one gains knowledge of death as a boundary of human life from the experience of other people's deaths. Whoever crosses that boundary does not return.

It is not a matter of subjective experience of the isolated Self to determine in what direction everyday life is transcended, how to interpret these acts of transcendence, and to understand and deal with them using symbols and rituals. Rather, this is an outcome of historical sociality of human existence, which is the primordial "anthropological" transcendence of our "biology." In other words, it depends on predefined social constructions of reality, of both the everyday reality and the extraordinary one.

The knowledge we call upon to say what was and was not "in reality," what exists "only" in the dream – that knowledge has its home in the natural attitude of daily life, and is, thus, bound to what is taken for granted there. The reality accent of daily life certainly always has practical priority in clear daylight, and under normal, secure circumstances. Night and dreams are excluded. Once the claim to reality of everyday life is reinforced by a theory of reality that denies the claim to reality of other areas of meaning, *a priori*, and is used as a basis for defining reality as such, dreams as well as other extraordinary provinces of meaning appear as unreal. Inversely, it is much more difficult to define everyday reality as unreal. Although such postulates were recurrently imposed in "theory," the influence they could exert on the everyday action of ordinary – religiously "non-virtuosi" – people has been quite limited.

The "contents" of social construction of reality, that serve the universally human religious function of inserting the subject in a history that transcends him or her, can vary significantly. More precisely, the core of these properties is shaped by the collective religious constructs of "another" or "extraordinary" reality. These constructs are based on the *communicative reconstruction* of subjective experiences of transcendence.

III. Social Construction of "Other" Realities

The reference to the social construction of "other" realities, apparently, departs from the proto-social level of subjective experience of transcendence. Returning to this question is necessary to consider how subjective experiences of transcendence are "coped with," objectified, and then found the basis for social constructions of an extraordinary reality. As indicated earlier, two interconnected processes are involved, both implicating certain forms of *communicative action*.

The first operation consists of objectifying, verbally and symbolically, subjective experiences of different kinds of transcendence – ranging from "little," everyday instances to "great," extraordinary ones – by communicating them to others (or to oneself). In this process, subjective experiences of transcendence (more precisely, recollections of subjective experiences of transcendence) are reconstructed, usually *inter*subjectively, by fitting them into established communicative forms. The main types of such forms are symbolic references and markings, narratives which mythologize the experiences, and make them available for retelling, and rituals in which the experiences are commemorated. One could say that all three forms contain functions of the "collective" memory.

In the second of the aforementioned processes, the primary intersubjective reconstructions are already presupposed. They are treated as matters of dubitable character which need social control. First and foremost, they must be interpreted correctly, the interpretations must relate to each other so that they match (whatever "logic" may guide this match) and, where necessary, they need to be reformulated. Wherever this may be impossible, the experiences themselves – and not just their reconstructions – must be discarded. The systematization, thus, contains both a censoring selection, as well as canonization of correct interpretations. Where social claims to the relevance and the legitimacy of experiences of transcendence and their reconstructions are at stake, the relationship between ordinary and extraordinary reality can be "explained" in such a way that the social order of everyday life, including its institutions, is not endangered.

Obviously, one finds at this interface of realities a particularly strong potential for social change. There is, of course, a tendency for the "system" to tie back the norms that govern members' everyday action, and that serve to maintain the social order to meanings and values of an overarching "other" reality that legitimizes social order. Moreover, there is a tendency of the "system" to champion those "other" realities that allow this without too much difficulty. More precisely, it favors "other" realities that select and canonize intersubjective reconstructions of experiences of transcendence in a "system" preserving way. However, experiences of transcendences cannot always be successfully and completely domesticated.

Simultaneously maintaining the social order that rules everyday life – particularly in the realms of political power and economy – and of "another," only incompletely "legitimizable" reality, in any case requires complicated adjustment efforts: from creating interpretive intermediaries that allow compromise between "theology" and "popular religion" – ranging from different syncretistic devotional ceremonies to the creation of mediating "Third Orders" for laypeople – to the provision of enclaves for religious virtuosos – e.g., monasteries – up to the accusation of heresy and dogmatic destruction, or even physical elimination, of religious "fanatics," and their replacement with more mundane custodians of the transcendent.

Realities, ordinary or extraordinary, that gleam through the universally human experiences of transcendence, are imagined, dreamed, hoped for, and feared. They are, initially, reconstructed in intersubjective communicative action. If the subsequent process, the social construction of transcendent reality, turns fairly successful, they assume a permanent and – sooner or later – binding ontological status.

Of course, the distinction between these two processes is artificial. Speaking of "universal human experiences" of transcendence makes sense only in the context of phenomenological reduction, that is, a strict philosophical method which allows one to gradually uncover the constitutive foundational structure of human experience (cf. Luckmann 1973). Concrete experiences of transcendence are necessarily historical, however, and are therefore determined to a large extent – in form and content – by antecedent social constructions of reality, including those of the "other" reality. With this caveat, and with all due caution, one can identify an ongoing dialectic of both processes. *Logically*, the first one precedes. There would be no social constructions of transcendent *realities* without prior intersubjective *communicative* reconstructions of the universal aspects of recurring human experiences of transcendence. The historical selection, codification, and institutionalization involved in the second process presupposes the processes of the first. Strictly speaking, however, there are no such primordial antecedents since all human experience is historically located and molded. Concrete subjective experiences of transcendence are always oriented, to a greater or lesser extent, toward socially constructed, objectified models of such experiences. Therefore, these second processes and their results *empirically* antecede the first. In either case – the "dialectics" of both processes – the variety of subjective religious experiences is socially constructed, as is the variety of social facts with elementary religious functions.

IV. Signs, Symbols, Rituals

Thus far, we have used the term "objectivated signs and symbols" only to address the basic dimension of communicating experiences of transcendence and their social construction for some "other" reality (a "sacred cosmos"). We need to explain this term at least succinctly, because the primordial intersubjective experiences of transcendence are based, directly or indirectly, on this dimension when reconstructed as mythological narratives, as invocatory or commemorative ri- tuals. We can, more or less successfully, transcend the boundaries of experience by virtue of the general, elementary, relational structure of intentionality, which Husserl, who described it in detail, called *appresentation*. In appresentational relationships, as the term indicates, something which is *not* experienced directly *is* presented by means of that which is given in immediate presentation.

If that which is appresented merely happens to be not present now for contingent reasons, but can be experienced directly at any other time, we are dealing with the simplest kind of appresentations. These are the kind of appresentations that help us "cope" with the "little" spatial and temporal transcendences of experience. *Indications* (such as smoke denoting fire from afar, or a stench that portends a cadaver) and subjectively set, socially not conventionalized *marks* (such as blazes on trees or traces in the snow) help us surpass the boundaries of our present experience. Nothing about these "transcendences" goes beyond everyday life, and nothing about these indications and marks refers to a "sacred cosmos." However, coping with such everyday-life transcendences when interpreting indications or creating marks may, certainly, produce problems for which, traditionally, special techniques were developed, generally subsumable under the notion of magic.

Another level of transcendence is involved in the experiences of fellow human beings or, more generally, of an *alter ego* – which does not *necessarily* have to be human (cf. Luckmann 1970). The consciousness of the *alter ego* cannot be grasped directly, but only as it expresses itself, and only if it is incarnated in one fashion or another. The "highest," most adequate apperception of indirect experience of another being, however, implies that it communicates by means of signs. Using signs presupposes a certain conventionalization, and conventionalization presupposes social action – precisely that kind of action in which the transcendence of *alter ego* is originally represented. This is not the place to analyze the complex intersubjective constitution of signs in everyday life, nor to trace with any degree of precision the transformations – partly of a metaphorical nature – by which they can refer to objects and events not only in the ordinary reality of which we have direct evidence, but also to an *alter ego*, and even to realities which transcend everyday life (cf. Luckmann 1972). Signs, at any rate, refers to something which is not experienced directly, and which can never be experienced directly – the consciousness of an *alter ego*. Language as a sign system is, obviously, the most important instrument for intersubjective reconstruction of subjective experience – including those of transcendence – and the most important tool for the social construction of everyday-life and extraordinary realities. Only indications and recollections can be taken from "other" realities in everyday life. They are memories of experiences in various other states: from dream or states of heighted wakefulness which sometimes – besides occasional reversal into unconsciousness – characterizes ecstasy. After one returns to the reality of everyday life, those recollections, of course, are "pointers" to other realities. They are "translated" into language, interpreted systematically, and expressed in symbols. A variety of significatory meaning references, especially signs and symbols, but even more simple forms, namely indications and marks, help "bridge" the boundaries of immediate experience. They deliver "messages" across those boundaries by appresenting in present experience that which is relevant for, but is transcending, the experiential core. Indications and marks help one cope with the "little" transcendence of space and time. Signs, intersubjectively constituted and "conventionalized," serve to foster mutual understanding with others. They "bridge," albeit inadequately, the rift that separates one being from another. Ultimately, symbols are representations of another reality *in* the ordinary reality. They are used, e.g., in ritual performance, to transcend the boundaries to other realities, including the ultimate frontier.

Symbols are the most complex appresentational relationships. Just as signs point to the otherwise, i.e., directly, inaccessible consciousness of an *alter ego*, symbols also point to something that cannot be experienced directly at all. But they differ from signs in one important respect: they refer to something which belongs to a reality experienced as different from everyday life. In symbolic relationships, however, that which is appresented is not only absent (as in all appresentational relationships), and it is not only absent as a matter of principle (because the consciousness of *ego* and *alter ego* can only communicate, not become one), it is absent in a radical sense. It does not merely belong to a different part of the same, everyday reality, it belongs to a different reality *entirely*. Disregarding their symbolic content, the *material* vehicles of significations and symbolizations remain elements of everyday life. They consist of events and objects which are experienced in the fully awake condition of ordinary experience.

One may be on the way into a "different" condition, into ecstasy, or one may experience it on the return to the normal condition of everyday life. These, however, are transitional cases. When the border of reality-domains is crossed in experience itself, the symbolic relationship is dissolved. The "other" reality is then experienced by myself (presumably as "another" Self) in ecstasy, in dreams, in mystic union, and so forth "directly" – or so we are told by others, so we perhaps even seem to *remember* after we return into everyday life. The recollections, of course, are now "pointers" to other realities; they may become stabilized as symbols, as key elements of reportable recollections of such realities. If that which has been experienced in "another" reality should retain its consistency beyond the faint traces which it left in recollection, it must be consolidated by appresentational relationships, by marks and signs, which in this case additionally perform a symbolic function.

The consolidation of recollections of transcendence-related experiences normally employs language. There are many familiar examples of narratives of "other" conditions, of experiences of "other" realities in various genres of texts, and the respective types of oral (and in literate cultures, of course, also written) communication in many societies bear witness to the ubiquity of such experiences.

I need not go into detail here about the constitution and the sign character of symbols (e.g., the relative irrelevance of the nature of their vehicles; the unlimited communicability of symbolic meaning).[2] But I need mention a type of *action* that corresponds to symbols. Put formally, rituals are actions. Rituals may be considered the action-mode of symbols. More precisely: they are *social* actions, oriented toward others. However, those who are addressed through rituals cannot be experienced, interpreted, and dealt with as fellow human beings. These "others," toward whom ritual action is oriented, belong to a reality different from the one the acting person is part of (cf. Soeffner 1988). Generally, social actions which are not projected in anticipation of a response are one-sided, and actions which are, are reciprocal. Rituals, however, do not fit this simple categorization. On the one hand, they are social actions; they are intended to receive a response. In their original meaning for the actor, they are reciprocal. Whether they in fact receive a response is another question. It is a question which cannot be properly answered by an outside observer. The reason for this is quite simple. Neither the "questions" nor the "response" are governed by the ordinary pragmatic rules of communication in everyday life. The acting person who asks "questions" tries to follow the rules that he or she thinks are valid for communicating with other realms of reality. Ritual action is directed toward extraordinary reality. It is insignificant in the context of everyday actions and communication but bears symbolically meaningful relationship to the sacred cosmos – ritual action being the carrier of symbolization. Sacrifices, rites of passage, burial rites, and the like represent "ultimate" meaning that need no "mediating translations" into the profane contexts of everyday circumstances.

In different societies, knowledge about this reality is established in varying symbolic objectivations. In addition to ritual action, we must consider another aspect. The interpretation of a possible "response" is sometimes quite obvious, e.g., in the form of indications understood as "magic" (it rains after the dance). Frequently, however, the interpretation of "response" is successful only by virtue of symbolic appresentation. In this case, the appresenting element of symbolic action does not necessarily need be, in our sense, social action. Likewise, natural phenomena – such as thunder or fire – may be regarded as divine interventions. By controlling interpretations of "response," the "other" reality is, somehow, brought under control. Rituals are not just objectivations: Once objectified and brought under social control, they can be transformed by certain institutions into, more or less, independent stocks of special knowledge. This special knowledge serves as a guidepost for explorations of extraordinary realms of reality; it will be preserved by specialists, and can be applied for everyday life practical purposes of political power and economic interest.

V. Privatization of Religion

The addendum to this book, which was written and published so many years ago, is intended to expand the basic theoretical concept of religion and society on some points I consider crucial.[3] The ways in which some of these basic concepts were formulated back then – even more than my typological analyses of historical and contemporary social forms of religion – occasioned simple misunderstandings, as well as valid criticisms. Thus, in this addendum, I intended to improve or clarify that which demanded to be elucidated and corrected in the original wording. I hope that the remarks on the subjective experience of transcendence, its intersubjective reconstruction in communicative actions, on the social construction of "other" realities, and on the role of symbols and rituals in these processes fulfil these purposes.

There is, of course, also a need to improve and expand the application of this theoretical concept to the analysis of historical social forms of religion, and the analysis of the modern development of a new social form of religion. Nevertheless, I deem that the original thoughts pointed to something evident a quarter century ago for one whose view was unobstructed by theoretical misconstructions – in particular, that of different secularization theories. However, if I wanted to incorporate all of these amendments and precisions, I would have to write a new, substantially more empirical, book. I will not do this. At least, I will conclude this supplement with a few remarks on the contemporary situation of "the" religion in modern industrial society – those who prefer proceeding in epochs may read: postmodern, postindustrial societies.

Privatization of religion is the central part of the general privatization of life in modern societies. Privatization of life results – almost "logically" – from the high degree of functional differentiation in the social structure. In previously multifunctional institutions that were typically "located" within the kinship system, and that regulated social interaction in archaic as well as in traditional societies, a central function slowly acquired a dominant position. These institutions correspondingly lost most of the other functional components that originally constituted them. At the same time, institutions with similar functions coalesced into specialized domains. Subsequently, in contemporary industrial societies, institutions have become highly interdependent elements of social subsystems. The norms of each subsystem are *comparatively* independent of the rules that govern action in other subsystems. Depending on the area in which they are located, social interactions are subject to rather heterogeneous, instrumentally rational norms.

The functional segmentation of modern social structure decisively helped to discontinue the social construction of a taken-for-granted, obligatory model of transcendent reality. In Western societies, the *specifically* religious representations pointing to the "great" transcendences of life, historically were under monopolistic control (canonization, censorship) of the Christian churches. Today, the "market" of "sacred universes" is hardly limited to the traditional Christian, specifically religious, representations. Rather, they must compete with orientations pertaining to the various levels of transcendence that stem from the most diverse sources. The "commodity market" of transcendences is based on distribution via mass media – books, journals, radio, television – academies and seminars, soul-therapy centers, and vagabond gurus from all corners of the world. Moreover, specifically religious representations of "great" transcendences derived from traditional "sacred universes," accumulated in the World Religions' *musée imaginaire*, are not just competing with each other. They also rival models of life guidance deriving from reconstructions of this worldly transcendences. *The members of modern industrial societies may live in an (increasingly?) similar everyday-life reality, but this reality is no longer oriented towards an identical extraordinary reality.*

Starting with the most simple assumption, the coherence of modern world views that bind together every day and transcendent realities is apparently much weaker than that in archaic and traditional societies, to such an extent that one is inclined to state that there is no overlap whatsoever. In any case, synoptic social constructions that subsume subjective experience of different kinds of transcendence, or their intersubjective reconstructions, into submodels are extraordinarily heterogeneous. For several generations now, the traditionally Christian "sacred cosmos" ceased to be the exclusive "other" reality with which broad segments of the population interact. The traditional, institutionally specialized churches were unable to safeguard their monopoly, even concerning specifically religious issues. Moreover, modern consciousness has been decisively molded by collective representations deriving from social constructions of experiences of "intermediate" transcendence (nation, race, classless society, different kinds of "emancipations," etc.). In addition, concerns with the "little" transcendences, symbolized by solipsistic notions such as "self-fulfillment" and the like, have become widespread. Their derivation from romanticism, certain branches of philosophical idealism, and the more recent "depth psychology" is obvious. But what were marginal phenomena then seem to have become mass phenomena now, broadly characteristic of modern consciousness. The apparent tendency to shift intersubjective reconstructions and social constructions away from the "great" other-worldly transcendences to the "intermediate" and, more and more, to the minimal transcendences of modern solipsism may be considered as the "thematic" (cultural) correlate of (social) "structural" privatization. There seems to be a powerful "elective affinity" between the structural privatization of individual life and the "sacralization" of subjectivity that is celebrated in much of modern consciousness. Nonetheless, traditional religious orientations – whose centers are moralizing social constructions of experiences of "great" transcendences – have by no means vanished. But the social distribution of these orientations has a smaller basis, and the institutionally specialized social locus of these orientations, the churches, no longer represent the socially dominant form of religion. The churches have become institutions among other institutions. The legitimizing traditional religious orientations they transmit are eclipsed in modern consciousness by orientations referring exclusively, on variable levels, to this-worldly forms of transcendence: the nation, the people, social class (or their "overcoming"), family (or new partnership forms of "autonomous" Selves), the *alter ego* ("togetherness"), and the sacralized, largely self-sufficient, individual.

A wider range of smaller and larger social enterprises is involved in the social construction of various kinds of transcendence. As mentioned, the basic structure of this process is that of a demonopolized market (see Berger 1963) that, however, tends to be oligopolistic. Mass media are predominantly active here. The churches also compete in this market (from televangelism in the United States to papal voyages with ground kissing). They strive to partake in the process of modern social transcendence construction. But as monuments to an earlier epoch of institutionally specialized religion, they must balance restorative and fundamentalist tendencies. Moreover, semi-institutional, more or less "new" and more or less "religious" communities – in the traditional sense of the term – that try to intervene in this process have emerged. Social structure has ceased to mediate in a coherent and binding way between subjective consciousness with its experiences of transcendence, the communicative reconstructions of these experiences, and competing versions of "sacred universes." For better or worse, privatization, as the predominant modern social form of religion, must be characterized by what it is *not* rather than what it *is*: It is specified by the *absence* of generally plausible obligatory social models for the persisting, universal human experiences of transcendence.

Notes

1 Aspects of this postscript are drawn from other texts, where they are treated in more detail: Luckmann 1985, 1988, 1989; Schutz & Luckmann 1989.

2 Collaboration with Peter L. Berger on the book "The Social Construction of Reality" lay in the years between the first German edition (1963) and the English revised and expanded edition (1967) of *The Invisible Religion*; I knew about Schutz' thoughts on symbols and transcendence (cf. Schutz 1973), but I only started dealing with them systematically when I put together and elaborated on Schutz' drafts, articles and manuscripts for "The Structures of the Life-World" (Schutz & Luckmann 1973, 1989). Hans-Georg Soeffner (1989) undertakes a more thorough analysis. [See also Soeffner 1997.]

3 This resulted from my further systematic study of Schutz's theory of symbols and ideas elaborated there regarding the subjective experience of different transcendences.

References

Berger, P. L. (1963). A Market Model for the Analysis of Ecumenicity. *Social Research* 30(1), pp. 77–93.

Luckmann, T. (1970). On the Boundaries of the Social World. In M. Natanson, *Phenomenology and Social Reality. Essays in Memory of Alfred Schutz* (pp. 73–100). Den Haag: Nijhoff.

Luckmann, T. (1972). The Constitution of Language in the World of Everyday Life. In L. E. Embree, *Life-World and Consciousness: Essays for Aron Gurwitsch* (pp. 469–488). Evanston, IL: Northwestern University Press.

Luckmann, T. (1973). Philosophy, Science, and Everyday Life. In M. Natanson, *Phenomenology and the Social Sciences* (pp. 143–185). Evanston: Northwestern University Press.

Luckmann, T. (1985). Riten als Bewältigung lebensweltlicher Grenzen. *Schweizerische Zeitschrift für Soziologie* 3, pp. 535–550.

Luckmann, T. (1988). Religion and Modern Consciousness. *Zen Buddhism Today. Annual Report of the Kyoto Zen Symposium (The Kyoto Seminar for Religious Studies)* 6, pp. 11–22.

Luckmann, T. (1989). *The New and the Old in Religion. Contribution to the Symposium on Social Theory and Emerging Issues in a Changing Society*. Chicago: University of Chicago, April 5–8. In P. Bourdieu & J. S. Coleman, *Social Theory for a Changing Society* (pp. 167–182). Boulder: Westview.

Schutz, A. (1973). Symbol, Reality and Society. In *Collected Papers I* (pp. 207–356). Den Haag: Nijhoff.

Schutz, A., & Luckmann, T. (1973). *The Structures of the Life-World, Vol. I*. Evanston, IL: Northwestern Press.

Schutz, A., & Luckmann, T. (1989). *The Structures of the Life-World, Vol. II*. Evanston, IL: Northwestern Press.

Soeffner, H.-G. (1988). Rituale des Antiritualismus. Materialien für Außeralltägliches. In H. U. Gumbrecht und K. L. Pfeiffer, *Materialität der Kommunikation* (pp. 519–546). Frankfurt am Main: Suhrkamp.

Soeffner, H.-G. (1989). Emblematische und symbolische Formen der Orientierung. In H.-G. Soeffner, *Auslegung des Alltags – Der Alltag der Auslegung. Zur wissenssoziologischen Konzeption einer sozialwissenschaftlichen Hermeneutik* (pp. 158–184). Frankfurt am Main: Suhrkamp.

Soeffner, H.-G. (1997). *The Order of Rituals. The Interpretation of Everyday Life*. New York: Routledge.

NAME INDEX

SUBJECT INDEX